## Contents

Unless otherwise noted all Scripture quotations are taken from the King James Version of the Bible.

All Scripture quotations marked RSV are taken from the Revised Standard Version.

All Scripture quotations marked Goodspeed are taken from **The New Testament, an American Translation** by Edgar J. Goodspeed.

All Scripture quotations marked Moffatt are taken from **The Bible, a New Translation** by James Moffatt.

1449
Broadman Press
Nashville, Tennessee

Designed by Ron Martin

Meet Southern Baptists

© Copyright 1978 ● Broadman Press.
All rights reserved.
4265-34
ISBN: 0-8054-6534-0

Dewey Decimal Classification: 286
Subject heading: SOUTHERN BAPTISTS

Library of Congress Catalog Card Number: 78-52960

Printed in the United States of America

# Baptist Roots

The people of God are always moving forward, to new places, to new experiences, and to new times. They move under God's leadership, claiming other lands and other people for his kingdom. Abraham heard God calling, "Go from your country and your kindred and your father's house to the land that I will show you" (Gen. 12:1, RSV); so he moved from Uz to Hebron. Jacob heard God speaking to him at Bethel in the night in a dream. He moved on to Peniel, where he struggled with the Lord face to face. Then with his family he moved to Shechem and finally to Egypt. His whole life was a long pilgrimage. Moses was at Horeb when he heard God's call to go to Egypt and lead the children of Israel out of bondage. Moses led them from the Nile River, across the Red Sea, to Mount Sinai, and finally to the Jordan River. Joshua then led them across the Jordan into Canaan.

God calls his people to look forward, never backward except for inspiration. Abraham never returned to Uz. As far as we know, Jacob never went back to Peniel. He did go back to Bethel for renewal, but only for a short time. Then he pitched his tent beyond the tower of Eder, looking ahead. Moses never returned to Egypt; and even when he fell on hard times in the wilderness of Zin, he knew that the abundant cooking pots of Pharaoh also carried with them penalties of bondage. Looking backward is not possible for a people of conquest and victory. Lot's wife did look back to Sodom and turned into a pillar of salt.

Baptists are among the people of God. Their roots go deeply into the Old Testament. They accept the whole Bible as God's own book for man. They believe resolutely that "In the beginning God created the heavens and the earth" (Gen 1:1, RSV). Their prayers are filled with the spiritual insights of the Psalms, and their ethics are shaped by the Law and the Prophets. Their worship is conditioned by the

Baptists are deeply rooted in the Bible, including the Old Testament. Long ago many inspired writers like Jeremiah and Baruch labored to put in writing the word of God to man (Jer. 36:4).

awesome proclamations of men like Amos and Jeremiah, and their feeling for the religious community is influenced by the singular devotions of men like Hosea and Isaiah.

Standing with spiritual feet firmly planted in the Old Testament, Baptists moved forward to the New Testament and move now from the New Testament always into tomorrow. Like Abraham and Jacob's lives, the Baptist way is a long pilgrimage in answer to the call of God.

Baptists know that denominations can turn to pillars of salt, too, and that only as they look forward to new fields and new challenges will they find their true place in God's marvelous plan for the world. With roots firmly planted in the old traditions, it is the movement forward that keeps Baptists in touch with the new times and new challenges. This is in keeping with the spirit of Jesus Christ, who came to the world to make all things new. "Therefore if any man be in Christ, he is a new creature: old things are passed away; behold, all things are become new" (2 Cor. 5:17).

Baptists believe that the world is renewed through the spiritual rebirth of the person and that revitalization comes in deciding to renounce wrong and to accept Jesus Christ as the Lord of life. Decision is only the door. The renewal is the inner presence of the Spirit of God. As individuals are reborn, the world is renewed. This is one reason Baptists place so strong an emphasis on evangelism. Renewal in Jesus Christ is good news. Evangelism is the joyous announcement of that good news to the world.

It is from Jesus himself that Baptists take the shape and form of church life. With other Christians they confess that he is the Christ, the Son of the living God. This confession is the rock of their faith. They accept as eternal truth the response of Jesus to Peter's confession of faith: "On this rock I will build my church, and the powers of death shall not prevail against it" (Matt. 16:18, RSV). For Baptists the church is a divine institution—impregnable, indestructible, and triumphant. It has a mighty mission: "That through the church the manifold wisdom of God might now be made known to the principalities and powers in heavenly places" (Eph. 3:10, RSV). That it is triumphant cannot be denied. "Unto him be glory in the church by Christ Jesus throughout all ages, world without end" (Eph. 3:21).

As a movement of the people of God the church goes on and on, striving hard for the

Jesus Christ announces the church to his disciples. Peter confesses Jesus as the Messiah. Jesus responds by saying, "On this rock, I will build my church, and the powers of death shall not prevail against it" (Matt. 16:18, RSV).

faith of the Scriptures and always finding new ways and new words to declare the truth of God: "To make all men see what is the fellowship of the mystery, which from the beginning of the world hath been hid in God, who created all things by Jesus Christ" (Eph. 3:9).

If the announcement of the church was made at Caesarea Philippi when Jesus said he would build it on the confessions of his people, the church came into power on the day of Pentecost when the Spirit of God fell as tongues of fire on the praying disciples.

Pentecost was a day of decisive movement: first the people moving together in prayer, then the Holy Spirit moving in their midst, and finally three thousand souls moving into the church in response to Peter's mighty sermon. The church began as a forward movement of the people of God.

The book of the Acts of the Apostles is a sweeping record of their preaching and their works, a model for Baptist work and life. At the beginning a small group of uncertain disciples were debating the nature of God's kingdom. They were nondescript and unknown, a tattered band of outcasts. Even at Pentecost mockers said of them, "They have had too much new wine" (Acts 2:13, Goodspeed).

"New wine" indeed it was, but not the kind familiar to the mockers. These strange believers were filled with a new spirit and a new challenge. Jesus Christ within them was the strong "new wine" of their lives. They were beginning to understand what Jesus meant by his words "You shall receive power when the Holy Spirit has come upon you; and you shall be my witnesses in Jerusalem and in all Judea and Samaria and to the end of the earth" (Acts 1:8, RSV). The "new wine" went to their hearts; and they were ready to give themselves for the renewal of the whole world, an impossible task in the eyes of their enemies.

For these early believers Jesus Christ was supreme. Though "born of woman" (Gal. 4:4), he was before Abraham (John 8:58) and even before the foundation of the world (Eph. 1:4). In fact, he was in the beginning with God and was of the Godhead himself (2 Cor. 5:19). These Christians steadfastly held that Christ was crucified, buried, and resurrected. The members of the first church were among those who had seen him after his resurrection, and the preaching of the resurrection became central in the proclamation of the church.

The people of God moved forward by

"Take, eat; this is my body" (Matt. 26:26, RSV). With these words Jesus instituted the Lord's Supper, one of the only two ordinances of the church.

preaching and by personal testimony. Peter and John were jailed for their sermons, released, and jailed again. But the fellowship grew, and soon it was necessary for the church at Jerusalem to name seven laymen as special helpers to the apostles. One of these, a man named Stephen, full of the faith, died a martyr. He was stoned to death for preaching the good news. None of the discouragements stopped the aggressive work of the early believers.

Many years later one of their leaders, the apostle John, had a vision of the early Christians who had been victors over tribulation imposed by Satan. The angel told John, "They overcame him by the blood of the Lamb, and by the word of their testimony" (Rev. 12:11). The people of God most surely have prevailed when the life, the death, the burial, and the resurrection of Jesus Christ were proclaimed and when believers told others what he meant to their lives.

Soon the Christians had become vigorous enough to bring organized persecution from their enemies. One of the chief persecutors, a highly educated man named Saul of Tarsus, was himself converted. With a new name he quickly became Christianity's strongest defender of all—the Christian movement's first intellectual and probably its first missionary. Paul moved from city to city preaching to Jews and Gentiles, common men and kings, and at last dying in prison in Rome. But even in death his eyes were set toward Spain, in his day one of the ends of the earth. The Acts of the Apostles closes with Paul in Rome "preaching the kingdom of God and teaching about the Lord Jesus Christ quite openly and unhindered" (Acts 28:31, RSV). By then the direction and the form of the church had been well set, having several very clear and distinguishing marks, understood by Baptists to be about as follows:

• The church is the body of Christ in the world and is responsible for his work.

• The church worships through the reading of the Scriptures, the spoken word, prayer, hymns, the Lord's Supper, and baptism.

• The church proclaims the good news of Jesus Christ by preaching his death, burial, and resurrection.

• The church confronts the world through the teaching of the Scriptures.

• The church witnesses to the saving power of Christ through the daily walk and testimony of its members.

• The church ministers to the needs of its members and its neighbors.

• The church applies the teachings of the Scriptures to all the social and ethical problems of life.

• The church mingles in the marketplace and makes no distinctions between people, but through self-discipline it keeps itself clear of the evils of the world.

• The church divides and grows.

• The church has no inferior or superior members; all do the work and all share the honors.

• For the church "the field is the world" (Matt. 13:38).

During New Testament times the churches closely followed this pattern. The first churches in Jerusalem and Antioch and the later ones in Ephesus, Corinth, and Rome were all free congregations. But later as the work grew and became stronger, the churches institutionalized by becoming rigid in form and practice. By the fifth century A.D. many of the simple New Testament teachings had become creedalized. The people of God became more of an establishment and less of a movement. They grew by organization and regimentation and not by the free movement of the Holy Spirit in the hearts of men.

For a thousand years the spirit of freedom was partially buried under layers of forms, creeds, laws, decrees, protocols, and ceremonials. The churches became "The Church," and as it grew rich it became political and secular. The freedom to be found in Christ was not a vital part of the experiences of all the members. To many of them his words "Ye shall know the truth, and the truth shall make you free" (John 8:32) were meaningless. Paul's magnificent concept of the "glorious liberty of the children of God" (Rom. 8:21) was lost to most people.

But there were many valiant believers who fought hard to keep the free faith alive, although some of their doctrines and practices would be foreign by current Christian standards. Among the earliest were the Novatianists, the Donatists, the Paulicians, and the Cathari. The Novatianists believed in the strict enforcement of church discipline for the sake of a pure congregation. The Donatists held a rigoristic morality and rebelled against the dominance of the church at Rome and the emperor of the Roman Empire. The Paulicians stressed the holy life and opposed the special consecration of ministers and the system of church hierarchy. The Cathari emphasized the spiritual life and worshiped in preaching and prayer. They had little to do with rites and ceremonies.

A later group were the Waldenses, "the poor men of Lyons," the followers of Peter Waldo. A wealthy merchant, Waldo became so concerned that he renounced his riches and became a poor man in order to identify with the masses. The Waldenses were simple preachers. They opposed the offering of the Mass, the excessive wealth of the church, the teachings on purgatory, the worship of saints, and the hierarchy. They lived by the Sermon on the Mount, and they preached repentance and conversion.

8

The very first thing the early church did after the Holy Spirit came into the midst of it was to proclaim Christ as the risen Savior. This was done through a sermon preached by Simon Peter (Acts 2:14-36, RSV).

Then in England came John Wycliffe and the Lollards. Wycliffe and his helpers produced the first Bible translated into English. He was the author of pamphlets which were widely read and held that the Bible alone is necessary for the guidance of faith. Wycliffe also taught that only the called in Christ are the true members of the church. So fierce were the leaders of the established church against Wycliffe and his ideas that they burned all of his writings. Even years after he was dead, his bones were exhumed and burned at the stake.

The Lollards were the lay preachers of Wycliffe's ideas. They were peaceful Bible-reading believers who quietly taught true freedom to be found in Jesus Christ. Though persecuted and cast down, the ideas of Wycliffe and the Lollards prevailed and became a part of the faith of the whole English-speaking world.

Next were the thundering voices of the Reformation (1517-1648), Martin Luther preaching justification by faith, John Calvin preaching the high calling of God, and John Knox preaching man's freedom in Christ. In the background were the Anabaptists, who advocated a highly spiritual Christian fellowship and who held together in rigorously disciplined separate communities.

Baptists are indebted to all of these persons and groups and to many others, especially to men like Felix Mantz and Balthasar Hubmaier. Mantz refused to baptize his children before they were old enough to understand their profession of faith and was drowned for his convictions. Hubmaier held that it is the right of all men to follow their own "inner light" to serve their country as free citizens. He defended the idea of the free church at the cost of his life and was burned to death for his faith.

These men and groups were not Baptists, and some of them held ideas which Baptists today deem unacceptable; but to them Baptists owe a great debt. Through the centuries

Puritanism and a rebellion against the excesses of the courts of Henry VIII and Elizabeth I.

In the midst of this turmoil a vigorous group of Christians called Separatists broke out of the Church of England because they regarded its leaders as false in doctrine and corrupt in practice. Naturally, these leaders opposed the Separatists and all other free church groups.

Everywhere new life was emerging. The yeast was growing, and new allegiances were forming. The working of God's Spirit had wrought fundamental change. Among the free church defenders some very clear ideas were coming together:

1. The need for church members to have Christian experiences

2. The subordination of organization and structure to secondary positions

3. An equalitarian church life with members in democratic control

4. A single ethical standard for all members, pastors and people alike

5. Freedom or voluntarism in church membership

6. The absolute authority of the Scriptures in matters of faith and practice

7. Lay participation in the leadership of the church

8. An emphasis on the religious liberty of all peoples

9. A feeling that infant baptism was contrary to the teaching of the Scriptures

10. Jesus Christ as the only head of the church.

Out of the seething turmoil and these ideas Baptists were born. Their life-giving roots went deep into the subsoils of history. A new kind of congregation was coming into existence, one which would be defended by its founders and members as more truly representative of the churches of the New Testament. The dawn of the seventeenth century saw the beginning of the Baptists among a small group of English exiles living in Holland.

they kept alive simple New Testament ideas that Baptists have since come to cherish and defend. The Lollards, for example, stressed the laymen's responsibility of the church. Hubmaier believed devoutly that Christians should be loyal to the government. The Anabaptists were among those responsible for developing the free church principle which held that the church is composed of lay people in corporate community, in which the Holy Spirit is present. John Wycliffe magnified the importance of the Scriptures, and Martin Luther and John Calvin opened the way for our understanding of salvation by grace.

At the end of the sixteenth century all of Europe was in great religious turmoil. Christendom was in ferment, and this feeling was fostering unprecedented spiritual revival that would later call out the Baptists to take their proper place in the Christian world. Reformation was well under way. The Anabaptists were influential especially in Germany and the Netherlands, and to some extent in England. The new Church of England was shaken by

# Baptist Witness Through the Years

John Bunyan, early Baptist pastor and author, was imprisoned fourteen years for preaching his faith. He wrote **The Pilgrim's Progress**, a Christian classic still widely read.

**M**ost church bodies have great historical heroes whose theological works are still carefully studied as part of their heritage. Baptists have none. Lutherans have Martin Luther; the Reformed have John Calvin; and the Methodists have John Wesley. To a lesser extent the Presbyterians have John Knox and the Anglicans have Thomas Cranmer. Most of these men were the founders of their churches.

Baptists have only a few fleeting figures, some of them bearing the Baptist name only for brief periods yet influential in Baptist life. One of these was John Smyth, the founder of the first Baptist congregation in Holland. He was an exile from England, having fled with other English Separatists from the harsh persecutions of James I. Educated at Cambridge University for the Church of England ministry, he fell under Puritan influence while still a student. After preaching a short time in Lincoln, he despaired over the harshness of the established church and retreated to northern England, where he worked as a physician and helped organize a Separatist congregation.

God's Spirit was hovering over his people as a cloud, and they were moving as he moved. Because of continued persecutions, Smyth's church migrated to Holland. There in 1609 Smyth clearly enunciated what later became some of the primary principles of the Baptist faith. One of them was that baptism should not be accorded to infants, but only to believers old enough to understand the meaning of their professions of faith. So in Leyden, Holland, John Smyth baptized himself and then other members of his Separatist congregation to form the first Baptist church.

Smyth was impressionable and soon was fascinated by some of the extreme views of the Mennonites. After a period of study and negotiation he applied for membership in the Waterlander church. Before he could be admitted he died from tuberculosis. Most of the members of his church later joined the Mennonites.

Less than a dozen men and women were left to defend the ideas of this early Baptist body. One of these was a lawyer, Thomas Helwys, who had been educated in Gray's Inn in London. He felt that Smyth was wrong on several points. Smyth doubted the validity of his self-baptism. He believed that Christians should not serve the government or the military. By turning to the Mennonites Smyth seemed to withdraw from the world. Helwys thought that these doubts were inconsistent with Christian freedom and Christian citizenship. He strongly believed that the best place for the Christian was in the society he was seeking to win.

**11**

*Heare, o King j, and dispise not y counsell of y poore, and let their complaints come before thee.*
*The king is a mortall man, e not God therefore hath no power over y jmmortall soules of his subjects, to make lawes e ordinances for them, and to set spirituall Lords over them.*
*If the king have authority to make spirituall Lords e lawes, then he is an jmmortall God. and not a mortall man.*
*O king, be not seduced by deceivers to sin so against God whome thou oughtest to obey, nor against thy poore subjects who ought and will obey thee in all thinges with body life and goods, or else let their lives be taken from y earth.*
*God Save y King*

*Spittlefield neare London.*                *Tho: Helwys j*

the king must not try to control their religious lives.

He was immediately thrown into jail for his views. The congregation he founded was known as a General Baptist church because it rejected the Calvinistic idea of selective atonement, claiming instead that Christ died for all men alike, not just the elected. This was a view sometimes called Arminianism. Helwys' congregation continued almost into the twentieth century.

About 1640 a new kind of Baptists emerged. They were dedicated to Calvinistic principles. Known as Particular Baptists because of their views on the atonement, they had seven churches in the London area by 1644. Much more vigorous than General Baptists, the Particular Baptists grew rapidly and soon became a major influence in English life.

London Baptists formed themselves into an association for the purpose of closer fellowship. Their first act was to frame a Confession of Faith, the first of many such confessions later written by other Baptist groups.

The

CONFESSION

OF FAITH,

Of those CHURCHES which are commonly (though falsly) cal led ANABAPTISTS;

Presented to the view of all that feare GOD, to examine by the touchstone of the Word of Truth: As likewise for the taking off those aspersions which are frequently both in Pulpit and Print, (although unjustly) cast upon them.

Acts 4. 20.
*Wee can not but speake the things which wee have seene and heard.*
Isai. 8. 20.
*To the Law and to the testimony, if they speake not according to | this Rule, it is because there is no light in them.*
2 Cor. I. 9, 10.
*But wee had the sentence of death in our selves, that wee should not | trust in our selves, but in the living God, which raiseth the dead; | who delivered us from so great a death, and doth deliver, in whom | wee trust that he will yet deliver.*

LONDON
Printed by *Matthew Simmons* in *Aldersgate-street.*
1644.

Helwys decided to lead his little band back to England. He had become convinced that one ought not to withdraw to a foreign land because of persecution. So in 1612 God's Spirit moved, and the Helwys band moved with him across the stormy English Channel to Spitalfields, near London, where that year the first Baptist church on English soil was organized.

One of the first things Helwys did was to write a pamphlet, "A Short Declaration of the Mistery of Iniquity," pleading for freedom of conscience. This was the first demand made for religious liberty in England. In a kind of open letter addressed to the king, Helwys said: "The King is a mortall man, e not God, therefore hath no power over ye immortal soules of his subjects, to make lawes e ordinances for them, and to set spiritual Lords over them." Helwys believed that Christians should work willingly for the government and even should serve the king in arms, but that

From that time forward they dominated General Baptists. Finally in 1891 the two groups merged.

Particular Baptists became greatly concerned over what they felt were doctrinal impurities among the free churches, especially among the General Baptists and the Anabaptists. So in 1644 the seven churches of London formed an association for the purpose of writing a confession of faith. They wanted to state clearly their convictions on the atonement and other basic ideas.

Three men were widely influential in early Particular Baptist life. The first was a layman, William Kiffin (1616-1701), a wealthy wool merchant who got his start in Holland while exiled for his faith. Learned in theological matters, he often debated with ministers and was one of the framers of the 1644 confession. Two of his grandsons, William and Benjamin Hewling, were hanged, dying (it was said) "for English liberties and the Protestant religion."

Hanserd Knollys (1599-1691) was a pastor, scholar, and teacher. He published Hebrew, Greek, and Latin grammars and was frequently involved in religious debates. His great learning helped deny the early charges that Baptists were unlearned and illiterate.

Benjamin Keach (1664-1704) was a tailor, self-educated and self-employed, who also served as a Baptist minister. He was publicly tried for having taken "damnable positions contrary to the book of Common Prayer." His church was the first in all of England to use modern hymns as distinct from psalms paraphrased and set to music.

These early leaders, including even John Smyth and Thomas Helwys, are barely known to modern Baptists. None have the status and the learning of Martin Luther or John Calvin. Perhaps for Baptists, because of their tendency to shun creeds and other kinds of final statements of doctrine by mere men, it is very difficult for any leadership to become absolute above all other points of view. Baptists tolerate heroes only as long as they do not rise above the people or become too preoccupied with their own opinions. Baptists are willing to accept their heroes as great inspirational leaders, but not as final authorities. In some ways this self-reliance accounts for the vigorous life of small Baptist congregations. Much Baptist ministry is lay in character and will not be intimidated by the pretensions and absolutes of merely mortal men.

Dr. Rufus M. Jones, a Quaker scholar,

The First Baptist Church of Providence, Rhode Island, may have been the first Baptist church in America. It was organized in 1639 and still exists. Its building is called a meetinghouse.

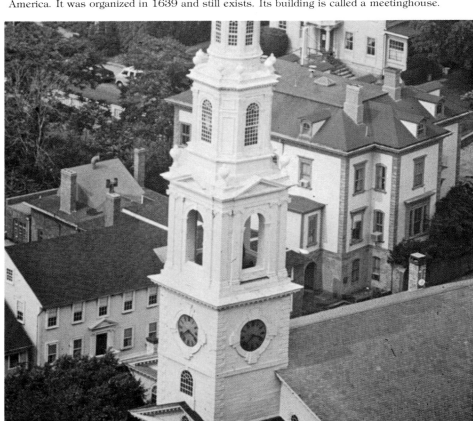

Perhaps the oldest Baptist church in the South is the First Baptist Church of Charleston, South Carolina. Its building dates from colonial times.

once said of early Baptist ministers that there were among them preachers who had been tailors, leather-sellers, soap-boilers, weavers, and tinkers. "The important point is that these preachers carried conviction and wrought righteousness and constructed spiritual churches to the glory of God. They did in their generation, what herdsmen and vine-dressers did in the early days of Hebrew prophecy, what tax-collectors and fishermen did in the primitive days of the Church; and it was vastly to the credit of these primitive Baptists that they rediscovered how to bring the gifts of laymen and unschooled members into play for spiritual ends."

Even in America early Baptist leaders were not men greatly renowned as theologians. Some were scarcely Baptist at all, especially as we now understand what Baptists stand for. Roger Williams was one of those who was associated with the Baptists for a brief time and who was greatly influential in both secular and Baptist life. Regarded by some as a layman, he spent most of later years giving leadership to the commonwealth of Rhode Island, which he helped form. He had been ordained a minister in the Church of England but was caught up with the Separatists. He immigrated to Boston, where soon he was in trouble with the authorities. He attacked them because of their persecution of other Christians and their dishonesty in dealing with the Indians.

He escaped in the cold of winter to Rhode Island. Here he briefly took up the Baptist position and made three great contributions to the Baptist heritage. He clearly enunciated religious liberty as a Baptist principle; he founded the First Baptist Church in America at Providence, in 1639. He demonstrated the right and privilege of Christian involvement in civic affairs. Soon after the organization of the Providence church in 1639, Williams left the Baptists and became a Seeker, unattached to any congregation.

For sixty years in America Baptist work made only moderate progress. In 1700 there were only ten churches in all of New England with not more than three hundred members. There were others in Pennsylvania and New Jersey and some in the South. By the beginning of the Great Awakening in about 1734 there were only forty-seven known Baptist churches in America, of which all but seven were in the North. One of the seven was the First Baptist Church, Charleston, South Carolina, established possibly as early as 1683 or as late as 1699. The founder is assumed to be William Screven, a wealthy farmer and merchant from Kittery, Maine.

But generally, for all of their simple principles, Baptists were not growing; and this was in times when other groups were rapidly developing. But with the coming of the Great Awakening God's Spirit began moving again. The people at once moved with him, and out of the moving Baptists began to multiply.

Under the preaching of Jonathan Edwards and George Whitefield a great revival broke out, sweeping church after church and bring-

**15**

Baptists came to America before many of the states were formed and before modern maps were made.

ing thousands to newfound faith in Jesus Christ. The conservative, preoccupied General Baptists were not impressed and took very little part in the Great Awakening. But as religious conversion was preached and new congregations were formed, some of the members (of other churches) became dissatisfied with the baptism of infants. Those disaffected organized still other churches that denied infant baptism, only to discover that they were similar to the Baptist churches in their neighborhoods. Almost overnight the Baptists grew like Jonah's gourd, according to one historian. These new congregations were called Separatist Baptists.

Among those who joined the Baptists was Shubal Stearns, a man of small stature with a big heart and expansive vision. Even while he was pastor of a Separatist church in Connecticut he declared against infant baptism and joined the Baptists.

Stearns was soon convinced that he should take the gospel to the western settlements. He was forty-nine years old, but age was no deterrent to keep him from launching his own personal bold mission thrust.

Stearns stopped briefly in Virginia; then with eight families he led a pioneer mission service corps on to Sandy Creek, North Carolina. Here in 1755 he established the Sandy Creek Church, and in three years there were three churches with nine hundred members. In seventeen years the Sandy Creek Church organized forty-two other churches and sent out 125 ministers. Stearns was a preacher of

unique power and with a manner of preaching thought to have been widely imitated. He had a pleasant musical voice capable of arousing deep feeling. Of Sterns' work Morgan Edwards, a Baptist historian of the day, wrote:

"All the separate baptists [**sic**] sprang hence: not only eastward towards the sea, but westward towards the great river Mississippi, but northward to Virginia and southward to South Carolina and Georgia. The word went forth from this sion, and great was the company of them who published it, in so much that her converts were as the drops of morning dew."

In some ways Shubal Stearns with his fiery evangelism, his unlimited vision, and his genius of organization was the spiritual forerunner of Southern Baptists.

Virginia was settled by three different Baptist groups. The first were General or Arminian Baptists from England, who appeared in southeastern Virginia about 1714. The second group was from Maryland and settled the northern part of Virginia sometime after 1743. The third group were New England Separate Baptists, who settled the back country about 1760. None of these Baptists had an easy time, partly because of their fiery evangelism and partly because of their unwillingness to recognize any kind of authority. They were constantly in trouble with legal and ecclesiastical authorities.

North Carolina, like all other colonies, had dissenters—men who would not conform to the official church—from the beginning. In 1704, for example, John Blair, a minister of the Church of England, described some itinerant preachers—"ideal fellows who have left their lawful employment, and preach and baptize through the country without any manner of orders from any sect or pretended church." This is probably a reference to Baptists. The first church in the state was in Chowan County. It was organized in 1727 and two years later had thirty-two members.

The work in Maryland began in 1742 when Henry Sater invited itinerant Baptist preachers from Pennsylvania to conduct services in his home near Baltimore. That same year Sater deeded an acre of land for use of a congregation of fifty-seven members that had been organized in the community.

The first Baptists in Georgia settled about 1733. This was at the time the colony was opened for permanent settlement. It was not,

Representatives of five local Baptist churches in the vicinity of Philadelphia formed the first organized association of Baptists in America. The date was July 27, 1707.

Many of these early churches were Arminian in theology. This changed because of the influence of the church at Charleston, which had accepted the Philadelphia Confession of Faith that incorporated a moderately Calvinistic stand.

The formation of the Philadelphia Confession in 1742 is probably one of the most influential events in American Baptist history. It was also the product of America's first organized Baptist work.

Baptists first appeared in Pennsylvania in 1654 when Thomas Dungan helped establish a church near Philadelphia. An Irishman, Dungan had fled the wrath of English kings who were bent on destroying the Baptist witness in Great Britain. A second church was Old Pennepack founded by Elias Keach, son of Benjamin Keach, the famous London Baptist minister. This occurred in 1688.

Young Keach was not a Christian and offered himself as a minister as a kind of private

however, until 1772 that the first permanent church was established, at Kioka near Augusta. The second church appeared a year later at Botsford near Savannah.

The saying that Baptists grew like Jonah's gourd can be illustrated by what happened in the back country of South Carolina, along the ridge between the Enoree and Tyger rivers. In 1790 the Bethel church had 116 members; but in 1803 it had 390. In thirteen years it had tripled in size. Bethel Association, to which the Bethel church was related, grew from sixteen churches with 1,000 members in 1789 to fifty-two churches with 28,000 members in 1800. In 1804 this association lost nine churches to another association; yet because of increase by conversion, it had 828 more members than in 1800.

Baptists gained headway in America in the aftermath of the Great Awakening. This far-reaching revival had been fiercely opposed by the state church. Some evangelists were imprisoned.

Isaac Backus, a prominent Baptist pastor of Massachusetts, was employed by the Baptists of the Warren Association to make demands of religious liberty to the Continental Congress in 1774.

On June 4, 1768, four Virginia Baptist preachers and a layman were arrested for preaching. They sang hymns as they marched to jail.

joke. But at his first service he fell under conviction and was converted. After baptism he became a courageous Baptist leader. Under his care the Old Pennepack Church expanded to include many mission stations or congregations. By 1707 there were several thriving Baptist churches in the Philadelphia area.

In spite of the great simplicity of church life among the Baptists, there were many questions concerning faith and discipline. The leaders sensed the need for a general meeting of Baptists. Out of this need came the formation of the Philadelphia Association in 1707. Five churches participated in the organization. It was an association of messengers authorized by their respective churches to mediate and execute designs of public good and was modeled after associations in England and Wales.

The Baptist historian Robert G. Torbet says of it, "The Association was regarded as both an advisory council in matters of local concern and an expression of the larger church through which the mind of Christ might become known." Among other things, this association acted as a council for the ordination of ministers; and it examined itinerant preachers in order to protect the churches from impostors. Very early the association informally accepted the London Confession of Faith of 1689 as its norm. In 1742 it approved an adaptation of the London Confession and called it the Philadelphia Confession of Faith. The London Confession had been modeled

John Waller, a Virginia Baptist preacher, was whipped by the sheriff for preaching. Afterward, covered with blood, he preached one of his most powerful sermons.

Under cover of darkness, nine converts were baptized in the James River near Chesterfield, Virginia. Afterward the pastor was ordered to leave the county or face imprisonment. August 15, 1773.

after the Westminister Confession. The Philadelphia Confession formally became the central statement of faith of thousands of Baptist churches in the century that followed. It remained the unofficial norm of Baptist life until the writing of the New Hampshire Confession of 1833.

Religious liberty was one of the primary issues of Baptist life in early America. Roger Williams was its main light and opened the way for it to become one of the tenets of the Baptist faith. As early as 1690 Baptists in New England lost property because they refused to pay taxes for government support of the Puritan churches. This fight continued well over one hundred years and was one of the factors in the formation of the First Amendment of the United States Constitution.

Virginia Baptists especially suffered from violent religious persecution. First there was mob violence. Baptist ministers suffered from fightings, beatings, and whippings, frequently stirred up by the clergy of the official state church.

These spontaneous persecutions were followed by legal ones. Baptist preachers were formally jailed for disturbing the peace. One group was ordered to preach no more for a year. When they refused to obey, they were thrown in jail. In some instances Baptist churches were denied permits to erect meetinghouses.

It was during this period that several very strong and influential national Baptist leaders helped guide the development of the work. These were men especially known for their defense of religious liberty.

One of these was John Leland (1754-1841), a native of Massachusetts who lived for fifteen years in Virginia. Shrewd, witty, and eccentric, he was an able defender of religious liberty and a champion of Jeffersonian equalitarian political thought. Leland was not formally ordained and for ten years while pastor of a church near Culpeper, Virginia, was severely criticized for the omission of this formality. Finally he consented to be ordained with the laying on of hands. Noted as a writer of hymns and as a gospel preacher, he traveled widely from Massachusetts to Virginia.

It is thought by some that Leland was directly responsible for James Madison's introduction of the First Amendment to the Constitution. There is also a tradition that Leland once delivered the biggest cheese ever made by Massachusetts farmers to President Thomas Jefferson. When his wagon stopped and people gathered to see the big cheese, Leland preached piety and liberty.

Another stalwart Baptist defender of religious liberty was Isaac Backus of Connecticut (1724-1806). Converted in the Great Awakening, he became a Baptist for two reasons: Baptists would not baptize infants and Baptists stressed the internal call. He pastored one church for fifty years and became the first known employed agent of a Baptist group. He was chosen by the Warren Association to represent the cause of religious liberty at the Continental Congress. His chief concern was taxation for church support, which the Baptists fiercely opposed. Hugh Wamble, a Baptist historian, said of Backus, "Fortunately, Backus lived to see the First Amendment adopted, but, unfortunately he did not live to see the complete fall of the standing order in New England, even though he had laid his lethal ax to the root of that tree."

What were these early Baptist leaders fighting for? (1) For the right of the individual to practice and preach his religious faith according to his own inner light. (2) For the right of all churches to be free of government and ecclesiastical harassment. (3) For the right of the taxpayer not to be taxed for church support.

Early American Baptists had many other interests besides religious liberty. One was organizing new churches in unchurched communities. A leader in this work was John Gano of Philadelphia (1727-1803). When twenty-five years old he was sent on a kind of mission service corps expedition to South Carolina. It was the first of many such journeys that led him to Virginia, New Jersey, North Carolina, New York, and, finally, when he was sixty years old, to frontier Kentucky. He was one of the founders of Brown University in Rhode Island and was widely known for his preaching. Gano had an ingenious way of adapting obscure texts to current situations. On his way to Kentucky one of his boats overturned and much of his property was lost. On his arrival he preached from the text "so we all got safe to land." A vigorous, farsighted man, he must be counted as one of the first Baptist missionaries and, in spirit, the forerunner of thousands of dedicated pastors serving today.

Early in their life, Baptists in America began to emphasize the need for an educated ministry. Their first college was Brown University, established in Rhode Island in 1764. But in every colony there were Baptists who were dreaming of colleges.

One of these dreamers was Richard Furman of South Carolina (1755-1825), an early trustee of Brown and the man for whom Furman University in South Carolina is named. Something of a mental prodigy, Furman matured early and started his life's work at sixteen as a boy evangelist. He was ordained at eighteen and served one church for thirteen years; then he pastored the First Baptist Church of Charleston for the rest of his life. He also served as an itinerant evangelist and denominational leader. He was a devout patriot. So intense was his support of the American Revolution that Lord Cornwallis put a price of one thousand English pounds on his head. Furman was a defender of religious liberty and led in the fight to disestablish the state church in South Carolina.

The first of the great denominational organizers, Furman made significant contributions to associational, state, and national Baptist life. He was one of the founders of the Triennial Convention in Philadelphia in 1814 and was elected that convention's first president.

Furman's vision was far ahead of his time. More than any other person he helped shape the concept of the Southern Baptist Convention, organized twenty years after his death. He proposed a plan of operation for the Triennial Convention in 1814 that was not accepted, but it was so vital and practical that it became the plan for the Southern Baptist Convention at Augusta in 1845.

There are scores of others in this same fertile period of Baptist life who made creative contributions to the life and work of the churches. Their names are known, and their deeds can be read in the history books. But none of them can be pointed to as the founder of Baptist life.

Thomas Waford, a Baptist layman in Gouchland County, Virginia, was arrested for helping preachers in an evangelistic service. December, 1774.

Richard Furman, a powerful Baptist leader of colonial times, escaped the clutches of the British Army, who feared his prayers for liberty.

# Beginning of Modern Baptist Missions

By 1800 missions had become the dominant thrust of the Baptists. In the previous century four things had happened to bring this about. First, in the first decade the struggling churches in the Philadelphia area decided to organize themselves into a general Baptist body. From that time Baptists gained a new understanding of their polity: Local autonomous churches are stronger when they voluntarily cooperate in mission. The association became the pivotal organizational unit for denominational cooperation.

Second, the Great Awakening made thousands of Christians aware of the simple biblical beliefs of the Baptists. It also brought a new thrust in evangelism. As people realized that conversion should precede baptism, they were drawn to the Baptists, for whom this is a primary doctrine. Coming as they did from the warm fires of the great revivals, they were infused with the desire to win all the world to Jesus Christ. In some ways Southern Baptists particularly are still moving with the momentum that came to them in the Great Awakening.

Third, the westward expansion of America brought a new sense of missions. All along the frontier hordes of people were searching for new homes and new fortunes. This presented unprecedented opportunities for the establishment of churches. William Screven went to South Carolina, Shubal Stearns to North Carolina, and John Gano to Kentucky. Thousands of other leaders followed this early vanguard, leaving no person unevangelized or no community without a church. This spirit became a permanent part of the Baptist witness.

William Carey was the founder of the modern missionary movement. He served in India from 1793 to 1834. His program for missions was very simple: pray, plan, pay.

Fourth, Christian sea captains sailing to faraway India in 1793 found an Englishman working as a missionary, preaching the gospel, and translating the Scriptures: William Carey, who was sent by the Baptists of England as the first modern foreign missionary. The sea captains brought enthusiastic descriptions of his work to America. Some of them participated in the organization of mission societies to help support Carey's work. The new world vision rapidly grew. Even Baptist associations were caught up in a general enthusiasm for missions. In keeping with a tradition established by the Philadelphia Association early in the century, other associations began to send missionaries to the Indians and to the frontier.

James Leland, fiery Baptist preacher of Culpeper, Virginia. He is thought to have influenced James Madison in the formulation of the First Amendment to the United States Constitution.

Widow Wallace's home (upper left), where William Carey and Andrew Fuller led in the formation of the first foreign mission society in 1792. Kettering, England.

Carey was not alone in lighting the mission fires. One of the great missionary lights of all time was David Brainerd, a devout Congregationalist and the son-in-law of Jonathan Edwards. Brainerd gave his life to preaching to the Indians of New England. In all of this God's Spirit was moving, and once more the people were moving with it. New meaning was dawning for some of the great sayings of Jesus. At last the people were seeing that indeed "the field is the world" (Matt. 13:38) and that they were to "teach all nations" (Matt. 28:19). In 1814 Baptists were standing at the door of their greatest growth.

A single prayer meeting may have marked the future of Baptist mission more than any other event. It was held in a thunderstorm under a haystack on Williams College campus in Massachusetts in 1808. Out of it came a spirit and a dedication that moved Adoniram Judson and Luther Rice to give themselves to foreign missions. They were commissioned by the Congregationalists and sailed for India on separate ships in the spring of 1812. On their ways, they conducted private and intense studies of the Bible. Both men were independently convinced that they should become Baptists, and both were baptized on their arrival in India.

Their newfound allegiance to the Baptists left them without the promised Congregational support. The two decided that one should stay on the mission field, and the other should return to America to secure support for the new work. It was decided that Judson would go down into the well, and Rice would hold the ropes.

News of their decisions quickly got back to America, where from north to south there was a growing interest in organizing a convention for support of foreign missions. Rice began at once to correspond with Baptist pastors in America. He moved slowly on his trip homeward, stopping in South America and landing finally at Savannah, Georgia. At each stop there were letters waiting for him. They came in response to his plea for Baptist action. Again slowly he moved northward from Savannah, preaching and talking his dream of a convention for support of missions. Only thirty-one years old, he was aided by older men like Richard Furman of Charleston and Thomas Baldwin of Boston. The organizing date was set for May 18, 1814. Thirty-three delegates came from eleven states and organized "The General Missionary Convention of the Baptist Denomination in the United States of America for Foreign Missions," popularly called the Triennial Convention because it was to meet every three years.

The convention also organized the "Baptist Board of Foreign Missions" (later the Foreign Mission Society). Its first act was to elect Judson as missionary and Rice as missionary

Adoniram Judson (lower right) and his wife, Ann, were the first persons to serve American Baptists as foreign missionaries. They worked in Burma, beginning in 1813. Ann died in 1826. Adoniram served until his death in 1850. Luther Rice (opposite), who went to the mission field with Judson, returned to help form the Triennial Baptist Convention. He served as its first missions secretary.

agent. When the group adjourned, Baptists in America had come of age. They now assumed world responsibility. A torch had been lighted that burns brightly to this day.

Rice began at once to travel the length and breadth of the land, stirring up mission support and cementing together a vast mission spirit. His spirit was indomitable, as one of his letters shows:

"Since the date of my letter of the 19th of June, 1816, I have travelled 6600 miles—in populous and in dreary portions of country—through wilderness and over rivers—across mountains and valleys—in heat and cold—by day and by night—in weariness, and painfulness, and fastings, and loneliness; but, not a moment has been lost for want of health; no painful calamity has fallen to my lot; no peril

has closed upon me; nor has fear been permitted to prey on my spirits; nor even the inquietude to disturb my peace. Indeed, constantly has the favourable countenance of society towards the great objects of the mission animated my hopes . . . . I have, besides many other aids and liberalities, received for the missionary object, in cash and subscription, more than $4,000 . . . . The Lord hath done great things for us! Blessed be the Lord God, who only doeth wondrous things; and let the whole earth be filled with his glory."

The next year Rice traveled 9,359 miles and collected $5,443. In this way Baptist missions came alive. It rose from the work of the Holy Spirit. The people of God were again on pilgrimage but this time moving out to the entire world, swept along by God's mighty power. Baptists were learning an essential lesson: To engage in missions is to be sustained by missions. There was an urgency, as we can see from Rice's great letter. That urgency was present because Christ was present. Only as a denomination lives with Christ at its very heart can it go forward; and only as it sees the world as its field can it live with Christ at its heart. Else what meaning would there be in the words "God so loved the world, that he gave his only begotten Son" (John 3:16)?

John Lewis Shuck (1814-1863) was the first Baptist missionary to China, appointed first by the Triennial Convention in 1835 and reappointed by the Southern Baptist Convention in 1845.

Henrietta Hall Shuck (1814-1844), wife of John Lewis Shuck, was the first evangelical woman missionary to go to China and the second woman missionary to open a school in Macao for Chinese children.

Lott Cary (1780-1828), a resourceful black slave who taught himself to read. With the aid of friends he purchased his freedom and went as a Baptist missionary to Liberia in 1821.

ather Rice traveled the East Coast from Boston to Savannah sharing the vision of mission opportunities.

First Baptist Church, Augusta, Georgia, where the Southern Baptist Convention was organized in 1845.

The Triennial Convention at first had a single purpose—foreign missions. This can be seen in the preamble of its constitution, "for the purpose of carrying into effect the benevolent intentions of our constituents, by organizing a plan for eliciting, combining, and directing the energies of the whole denomination in one sacred effort for sending the glad tidings of salvation to the heathen, and to the nations destitute of pure Gospel light." Three years later home missions and education were added to the work of the Triennial Convention. These new additions were strongly opposed. Home missions did not become a firm part of the work until about 1838, and education was never seriously accepted.

Through this period some natural differences between Baptists of the North and the South were developing. Great distances, poor roads, uncertain mails, and natural geographical and social barriers greatly hindered free exchange of ideas and information. Yet somehow vast numbers of the people were able to move about. The years between 1814 and 1845 saw vast population shifts and social upheaval. For example, from 1812 to 1821 Kentucky grew 22 percent, Louisiana 41 percent, Tennessee 61 percent, Mississippi 81 percent, and Alabama 142 percent.

Slavery was greatly accelerated, as was the movement to curtail and abolish it. Great bitterness developed between North and South over the slavery question. Depressions, droughts, crop failures, and speculation added to the problems. The period from the formation of the Triennial Convention in 1814 to the formation of the Southern Baptist Convention in 1845 was one of the most difficult in the nation's history. It was also a time of opportunity. Baptists felt both the problems and the opportunities.

For example, this was the period when Baptist work began in earnest beyond the Mississippi River. In Oklahoma the first church was founded at Ebenezer Station on the Verdigris River by Isaac McCoy, one of the first Triennial Convention missionaries to the Indians. He left a meeting of the convention in Washington, D.C. in 1832 and by horseback traveled to Oklahoma. There on September 9 he organized the church with six members, half of them Creek Indians and half black slaves to the Creeks.

In Texas the gospel was preached by Baptists as early as 1822. The first church known to have been organized in Texas was constituted in 1837 at Washington on the Brazos by Z. N. Morrell. Nicknamed "Wildcat" because of his fiery and courageous nature, Morrell came from Tennessee and Mississippi to the new West. All of his life he worked for missions, going in his old age as a missionary to Central America. When he first preached on the Brazos there were fewer than fifty missionary Baptists in the state, but when he died in 1888 there were fifty thousand.

Other Baptist groups were also at work on the frontier. One primitive church under Pastor Daniel Parker moved intact from Illinois. Called the Pilgrim Church, it wandered about for thirty-four years and in that period organized nine new churches. There were other emigrant churches that moved intact into the pioneer areas.

Out of this great movement the Southern Baptist Convention was born, fully as much a missionary convention as the Triennial Convention before had been.

# One Sacred Effort

God's people were moving, and God's work was thriving in the South and the Midwest. Of this Torbet said, "Not only was the time favorable, but the Baptists had within themselves qualities and ideals which gave impetus to their progress. Their ministry, though frequently lacking in advanced formal training, was aggressively evangelistic; most of their ministers along the frontiers were unpaid and self-sacrificing men, and hence independent in the administration of their duties. Usually they were farmers or artisans during the week, and so shared with their congregations in the hardships of early American life."

Despite the great expansion and good fellowship between Baptists of the North and the South, there were problems that took root in the national social and political milieu. Beginning in the early 1830s slavery became a divisive issue. From the beginning many Baptists in the South were opposed to slavery. Associations passed resolutions against it, and frequently ministers spoke of its injustice and inhumanity. Some Baptists migrated to free states because they did not want to live in the midst of slavery. As late as 1832 it was not a problem in the Triennial Convention, but the next year things changed.

In 1833 English Baptists addressed American Baptists by saying, "Is it (slavery) not an awful breach of divine law? . . . Are you not as Christians . . . bound to protest?" This letter divided Baptists in America. This was simultaneous with the development of the abolitionist movement. Lines formed and tempers flared. By 1844 the Home Mission Society refused to appoint slaveholders as missionaries.

The difficulties became so great that in the spring of 1845 Virginia Baptists issued a call for a "consultative convention" of Baptists in the South. It was to be a "sectional" convention—a "full" convention, the call stated. The place was set at Augusta, Georgia; the date was May 8, 1845.

The leading figure was perhaps William B. Johnson (1782-1862), president of the South Carolina convention. In an address to South Carolina Baptists one week before the Augusta meeting, Johnson proposed a new convention. It would be different from the Triennial Convention organization. His proposal reflected the thinking of the late Richard Furman of Charleston, who had submitted a similar plan at Philadelphia in 1814. Johnson had been present at that meeting.

Robert Baker says of this proposal, "It is evident from this that Johnson was suggesting a different kind of denominational organization than the one utilizing the three autonomous benevolent societies as had been done heretofore. Disdaining the possibility of overwhelming the authority of local congregations, Johnson was suggesting a more centralized body that would have control over all the benevolent objects projected by Southern Baptists."

Churches in ten Southern states sent 293 delegates (later called "messengers") to the full consultative convention. The American Baptist Publication Society sent one corresponding delegate from Pennsylvania. There were no other representatives from the North. The cleavage between Northern and Southern Baptists was almost complete with the gathering of these people on May 8. It was completed when the delegates organized themselves into a convention along the lines suggested by Johnson.

The preamble of the new constitution was similar to the one adopted by the Triennial Convention in 1814—"carrying into effect the benevolent intentions of our constituents, by organizing a plan for eliciting, combining, and directing the energies of the whole denomina-

The central, basic book for all Baptists is the Bible. Their faith and practice must be in agreement with its precepts.

tion in **one sacred effort,** for the propagation of the Gospel."

The organizational heart of the new constitution was Article V, which incorporated the views of Furman and Johnson: "The Convention shall elect . . . as many Boards of Managers, as in its judgment will be necessary for carrying out the benevolent objects it may determine to promote, all which Boards shall continue in office until a new election. . . . To each Board shall be committed, during the recess of the Convention, the entire management of all the affairs relating to the object with whose interest it shall be charged." The primary purpose was missions, a fact clearly seen in the organization of two mission boards at the organizational meeting.

Almost at once, Southern Baptist churches renewed their devotion to missions. They proved again their New Testament purpose by incorporating into their names the word "missionary." They were not simply "Baptist churches" but "missionary Baptist churches." From this simple beginning developed the character and life of the Southern

Baptist denomination. They were missionary Baptist churches with purpose, destined to be drawn together in **one sacred effort**—a cooperative denominational enterprise that would preserve both the independence and the interdependence of the churches.

Much has been said about the independence of Baptist churches. They are local, autonomous, and free. They are independent of the government and independent of each other. Property is held in their names, and the deeds are in their own bank safety-deposit boxes. The churches call their own pastors and conduct their own work. Membership in the churches is voluntary, and cooperation of the churches with the general Baptist bodies is optional. They are free to join, free to withdraw.

In this, Baptists believe that they follow the New Testament pattern. As late as A.D. 96 the church at Corinth dismissed some of their elders installed by the apostles. The church at Rome appealed to it for reconsideration. There was nothing in the exchange to indicate that the Corinthian church had not acted within its

Benajah Harvey Carroll (1843-1914), a Baptist intellectual and spiritual giant; he wrote thirty-three books and founded Southwestern Baptist Theological Seminary.

rights or that the Roman church had any authority over the Corinthian church.

The independence of the churches was lost as bishops took the Roman Empire for their model. They visualized congregations everywhere in close affiliation, dominated by a council of bishops and finally by a prince. By the sixth century most churches were no longer free. They were held captive by a system that eventually would put all church property under control of the bishops and that would require obedience of all the members. Autonomous churches would become the absolute Church, and the Church and the state would be almost the same. The Church would be so powerful and authoritative that even kings would cringe in fear of it. From the fifth century, for a thousand years, free churches were renegade churches. They existed as obscure and clandestine fragments, awaiting the day when once again the Church would become churches and the churches would be free.

That day dawned on October 31, 1517, when Martin Luther nailed his ninety-five theses to the door of the Castle Church in Wittenburg, Germany. Though Luther himself never went the full distance in making the

churches completely free, his theses pointed the way to the Baptists and others like them who came in time to live autonomously and independently. The universal reign of the monarchical bishops was doomed.

But the independence of the churches is only half the story; the other half is interdependence. The New Testament teaches interdependence of churches just as clearly as it does independence. Congregations isolated and unrelated to other congregations are not true churches. True churches exist in relationship. The church at Antioch was related to the church at Jerusalem. Paul established a series of churches related to each other. Jesus addressed himself through John on Patmos to the seven churches of Asia, a family of congregations.

Cooperation is essential, and it is clear that churches that work together are able to accomplish more than churches that work alone. An isolated independent church may take a neighborhood for Christ, but only a community of related independent churches can take a city for Christ. The isolated church may make a big name for itself, but it will not win the world for Christ.

**31**

John Albert Broadus (1827-1895), towering intellect and denominational leader. His life was intertwined with Southern Baptist Theological Seminary and the Southern Baptist Convention.

Baptists derive their understanding of cooperation from the Bible, just as they do all of their other doctrines. The Bible for them is not just another sacred book. It is **the** sacred book, the book above all other books, God's own Word for man. It is God's revelation of himself given to the world through his own inspired apostles and prophets.

Baptists have long held a tradition of Bible study and Bible learning. Their greatest spiritual heroes have been champions of Bible interpretation and Bible preaching. One of the greatest of these was John A. Broadus (1827-1895), one of the founders of Southern Seminary and a New Testament scholar of extraordinary ability. Two of his greatest works are still in print. They are **The Preparation and Delivery of Sermons** and **Commentary on the Gospel of Matthew.** His great learning and his ability to make profound things clear and simple became a pattern for Southern Baptist preaching that has lasted even until this day.

Another Bible teacher of renown and influence was B. H. Carroll (1843-1914), who started his adult life as a skeptic. But after his experiences in the Civil War, he was dramatically converted in a Texas brush-arbor revival. He was twenty-two at the time. So rapid was his progress in the ministry that twelve years later he was asked to preach the annual sermon of the Southern Baptist Convention, a responsibility usually accorded older men. He served as pastor of the First Baptist Church, Waco, Texas, for twenty-nine years and as professor of theology and Bible at Baylor University for thirty-two years. In 1905 he organized a seminary at Baylor which about four years later became Southwestern Baptist Seminary.

Carroll was the author of thirty-three published volumes, including a thirteen-volume commentary. Gifted with a retentive memory and profound spiritual insight, he made a permanent impression on Baptist life. Like Broadus, Carroll still lives in the style of preaching followed by many Southern Baptist ministers.

In many ways these two men represent extremes of the Southern Baptist Convention. Broadus was a Virginian and was well educated in Eastern schools. He was a product of settled America and rose to the unusually high esteem of educated America. For example, he was the first Southern Baptist to deliver the Yale lectures on preaching, and his books are still widely used as seminary textbooks. Carroll was from frontier America, a product of the unsettled West, and became known for his rugged, direct manner. He too reached great

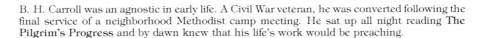

B. H. Carroll was an agnostic in early life. A Civil War veteran, he was converted following the final service of a neighborhood Methodist camp meeting. He sat up all night reading **The Pilgrim's Progress** and by dawn knew that his life's work would be preaching.

esteem and became the natural leader of thousands. Both leaders believed in the independent Baptist church, free and autonomous. Both men believed that independent Baptist churches thrive best in close cooperation with each other. Both men looked to the Scriptures for the light and revelation of God; and both men strongly believed that the Scriptures must be held central in the life of people dedicated to Jesus Christ.

It was out of this kind of conviction long present in Southern Baptist life that the Southern Baptist Convention was formed and was launched as **one sacred effort.**

It can be truly said that missions was the first **one sacred effort** of Southern Baptists. God's Holy Spirit was moving in the lives of his people, and they were joining in a new kind of cooperative movement. Though scarcely living outside the districts of their own birthplaces in their lifetimes, by giving themselves in prayer and by laying their means on the altar Baptists were moving out to the ends of the earth as God's people had never before moved. Cooperative mission work was born. It came from the hearts of the people.

Not all churches were missionary in heart, and not all wanted to cooperate. In fact, some were hostile and even malicious. They openly fought missionaries and conventions. Yet God's Spirit was so deeply at work that a new vital mission spirit was growing in the hearts of common people. One example is the Buckner family of East Tennessee. Caught up in the tide of rising mission conviction, Daniel Buckner began working in 1827 as a missionary in rural mountain communities, only to find open anger in some of the churches. The church of which he was a member excluded him for preaching missions. Mary, his wife, also asked to be excluded. The church replied, "We have no charges against you." Mary said, "If I were a man I would preach missions just as my husband has done, as I hope and pray my sons may do." The two turned to another church and were joyfully received on the statement that they had been dismissed for their mission conviction.

Henry Freiland Buckner (1818-1882) was a son of Daniel and Mary Buckner. After extensive education and ministry he set out for Oklahoma to become a missionary to the Indians. On a cold winter day in 1848 a crowd gathered at the Cumberland River boat landing to see his family off. His mother, Mary,

Annie Armstrong was one of the founders of Woman's Missionary Union and its first corresponding secretary.

said tearfully to him, "Go, my son, and the Lord be with you always. Our Saviour said, 'Go ye into all the world,' and it is as much my duty to give up my son as it is that of any other mother. I thank God I have a son to go to the Indians."

After suffering pneumonia at Nashville, Henry and Lucy Ann, his wife, arrived in Little Rock without money. He paid for his family's passage on a steamboat to Fort Smith by carrying wood for the boilers. In Fort Smith a Presbyterian friend extended hospitality. Buckner finally arrived near Fort Gibson on the Verdigris River in Oklahoma. He gave a note of forty dollars for a cabin in which a man had been murdered. And with only four and one-half dollars in borrowed funds, he used four dollars to buy a horse and fifty cents to employ a Negro interpreter to tell the Indians he had come to help them. He later said, "The first thing Mrs. Buckner had to do after walking four miles from the steamboat landing, leading our little son, was to scour the blood of the murdered man from the puncheon of our little cabin."

There have been thousands of Marys and Lucy Anns in Southern Baptist life, women who bravely gave themselves to missions. They have been an integral part of the one

sacred effort. Without them Southern Baptists would not be what they are today.

Two of them were Annie Armstrong and Lottie Moon, women of unusual character and Christian experience who became mighty symbols for Southern Baptist effort in missions. In a sense, Annie Armstrong "held the ropes" and Lottie Moon "went down into the well." Annie was an organizer and Lottie a missionary.

Lottie Moon (1840-1912) was born in Albemarle County, Virginia. Converted at nineteen in a revival conducted by Dr. John A. Broadus at Charlottesville, she taught school until 1873, when she volunteered for missionary service. This was in response to a sermon on the text "Lift up your eyes, and look on the fields; for they are white already to harvest" (John 4:35). She spent forty years in China. In 1888 she wrote a desperate appeal for more missionaries. This resulted in a Christmas offering for foreign missions that brought three new workers to the field. That offering has become a tradition in Southern Baptist life. In 1976 it reached an annual total of $28,763,810. The inspiration of Lottie Moon's life has been one of the offering's chief motivations. So scarce were funds that she once spent fourteen unbroken years on the mission field. In the midst of one of her deepest trials she wrote, "I hope no missionary will be as lonely as I have been." When the Chinese suffered famine, she starved with them. Literally starving, she became very weak and died aboard ship in Kobe, Japan, on Christmas Eve 1912. Her influence in the lives of Southern Baptist women is immeasurable. And because of her, hundreds have given themselves to foreign mission service.

Annie Armstrong (1850-1938) lived, wrote, planned, and spoke unceasingly for missions. Like Lottie Moon, she became a Christian at nineteen under the preaching of the great Baptist preacher and teacher Richard Fuller of Baltimore. Miss Armstrong was instrumental in the founding of the Woman's Missionary Union in 1888 and led in the framing of its constitution. Because of her clear vision and firm leadership WMU became an auxiliary to the Southern Baptist Convention. It did not undertake to raise money and send out missionaries independent of the Foreign Mission Board. In this way, Annie Armstrong preserved the great tradition of one sacred effort of the Southern Baptist people. This simple decision is one of the landmarks in Southern Baptist life. Had WMU been organized independently, the unity of the denomination would have been destroyed.

Miss Armstrong served also as the first corresponding secretary of Woman's Missionary Union, a post she held until 1906. For the last six years she refused a salary, until the WMU voted that the corresponding secretary must be paid. She was a tough, tireless worker, laboring long, hard hours and traveling distant miles. She once went eleven years without being out of the office a single day for illness. And in one twenty-one-day period, she visited nineteen places and spoke twenty-six times. In her honor the annual Annie Armstrong offering for home missions was established. It raised $9,575,851 in 1976. The WMU building in Birmingham is named for her.

Another woman of great dedication and zeal was Anne Luther Bagby (1859-1942), a missionary to Brazil. Born in Missouri, she moved to Texas with her father, who became president of Baylor College. Her thoughts were first turned to foreign missions by an African missionary. She soon became concerned for South America and with her husband, William Buck Bagby, went to Brazil in

1881. The Bagbys served as missionaries in Brazil for sixty-one years. Five of their children also became missionaries.

The continuing influence of one generation upon another is seen in the life of W. B. Bagby (1855-1939). He was converted under the preaching of Rufus C. Burleson (1823-1901), who very early in life had come under the influence of the rising mission spirit engendered by Luther Rice and Adoniram Judson. Leaving Alabama, Burleson turned to Texas as his mission field, where he became an outstanding preacher and educator. It was at Baylor, where Burleson served as president, that Bagby was converted. Young Bagby was also greatly influenced by B. H. Carroll in his first year of teaching at Baylor University. Then in turn Bagby himself became influential in the lives of thousands who became missionaries and supporters of missionaries.

For all those who are known and whose names are found in the history books, there are thousands of other less well-known figures just as dedicated and on whom the work depended. One of these was a farmer in Jack County, Texas. Converted after his marriage, he was taught to read by his wife so that he might better study the Bible. He became a Sunday School teacher and licensed exhorter. His role was to exhort the people on those Sundays when no pastor was present. This was in the rough depression period of the 1890s. At an associational meeting, missionaries presented their appeal. He left the room overwhelmed that he could not contribute. On his way home he prayed for a way to give. Looking down as he walked, he saw a fifty-cent piece half hidden in the dust. With joy he wept and returned to the room with his offering. This spirit can be illustrated thousands of times from the lives of anonymous men and women who gave themselves to missions.

While all of this was happening, the spiritual life of Southern Baptists was deepening, for, after all, mission and spirituality walk together. The old frontier revivals were rapidly disappearing, and a new evangelism was developing. The great educators and missionaries were also evangelists. John A. Broadus was noted far and wide for his fervent evangelistic preaching, and the seminary which he helped establish is still under the influence of his concern for the spiritual life of the masses. B. H. Carroll was himself an effective evangelist, and the seminary he established holds a chair of evangelism named after him. Carroll taught evangelism during the early years of his presidency. Because of their leadership and the leadership of men who came after them, the fires of frontier evangelism were burning everywhere, not just in the new towns and villages.

One great leader whose long ministry majored on evangelism was George W. Truett (1867-1944), who served as pastor of the First Baptist Church, Dallas, Texas, for forty-seven years. Born in the mountains of North Carolina, he moved to Texas in 1889 and was ordained in 1890. Without a college

**37**

J. B. Gambrell (**standing opposite**) and J. M. Frost formulate the final paragraph of a report to the Southern Baptist Convention recommending the establishment of the Sunday School Board. This agency publishes literature for the churches.

George W. Truett (1867-1944), renowned Baptist preacher. He was pastor of the First Baptist Church, Dallas, Texas, for forty-seven years.

degree he was employed to raise money for Baylor University. In twenty-three months he was able to free the school of debt. He then enrolled and was graduated in 1897. He soon became pastor in Dallas (1898) and served until his death. He preached in numerous revival meetings. For thirty-seven consecutive summers he was preacher in the "Cowboy Camp Meetings" of West Texas. He was the author of ten volumes of sermons, most of them evangelistic.

Truett was one of America's first great radio evangelists, and over the years he was the inspiration of other preachers in evangelistic and Bible conferences. An extremely broad-gauged man, he gave himself without stint to the denomination. His declaration on religious liberty spoken from the United States Capitol steps in Washington in 1920 is a classic statement. He supported B. H. Carroll in the founding of Southwestern Seminary and was himself one of the founders of Baylor University Hospital in Dallas. People who knew him best say that there was nothing petty or restraining in George W. Truett. He spoke a loud, sincere yes to Southern Baptist life. Above everything else he spoke a fervent, abiding yes to the evangelistic and spiritual life of the people and was one of the spiritual architects of the denomination.

Another noted leader was Edgar Young Mullins (1860-1928), educator, preacher, scholar, and denominational statesman, who served as president of Southern Seminary from 1899 to 1928. Born in Mississippi and educated in Texas, Mullins was a many-talented man. In early life he had been a railroad telegrapher looking toward becoming a lawyer. Called to preach, he offered himself as a missionary to Brazil. When this did not work out he became pastor of churches and for a time associate secretary of the Foreign Mission Board. Mullins was the author of nine important books, some of which are still studied in the seminaries. One of his major contributions to the thought of Baptists is composed of six simple statements called the "Axioms of Religion," which summarize Baptist doctrine in a most accurate way. They first appeared in 1908 in a book of that same title. The six axioms are:

"(1) Theological: the holy and loving God has a right to be sovereign; (2) Religious: all men have an equal right of access to God; (3) Ecclesiastical: all believers have a right to equal privilege in the church; (4) Moral: to be responsible, the soul must be free; (5) Religio-civic: a free church in a free state; and

Edgar Young Mullins (1860-1928), a denominational statesman, Baptist theologian, and president of Southern Seminary.

38

(6) Social: love your neighbor as yourself."

The influence of people like Broadus, Carroll, Truett, Mullins, Moon, and Armstrong made Southern Baptists what they are today. In 1845 at the time of the organization of the Convention membership stood at about 352,000. By the time George W. Truett ended his ministry in 1944 it had multiplied thirteen times. It doubled first sometime during the Civil War, and second in about 1877. It doubled again in 1917, 1944, and 1967. At the bottom of this expansion has been a great far-reaching evangelism—but not merely evangelism. Rather, it has been evangelism aided by broad, superior Bible teaching and enlistment programs. Again, at this point the Southern Baptist basic evangelistic objective has been strengthened by the **one sacred effort** purpose of the denomination. As cooperative enterprise, the Sunday School Board is one of the most thrilling developments in church and denominational history.

The lone person from the North present at the organization of the Southern Baptist Convention in Augusta in 1845 was a Pennsylvanian representing the American Baptist Publication Society, which had been organized in 1824. Already colporteurs and Sunday School workers were hard at work, principally in the West and South. The man was present in Augusta to guard the interests of the Society. It held publication and educational right of way in Southern Baptist churches until 1863, when the first Sunday School Board was organized. Even then it exercised considerable influence in Southern Baptist churches, an influence that may have increased in 1873 when the first Sunday School Board was consolidated with the Home Mission Board. Even though the Home Mission Board continued the publications, the influence of the Society was very great in Southern Baptist life—and because of this the present Sunday School Board almost did not come into existence.

The idea of the Sunday School Board was born in the heart and mind of James Marion Frost (1848-1916), the aristocratic and learned pastor of the Leigh Street Church in Richmond, Virginia. Later he described the beginning: "God touched me and I thought it." He proposed his thought in an article in the **Religious Herald** in February 1890. Both opposition and support followed. The 1890

Southern Baptist Convention established a Sunday School Committee instead of the proposed board. The Committee accomplished little except to recommend to the 1891 Convention the establishment of a board.

J. B. Gambrell (1841-1921), at the time the editor of the Mississippi **Baptist Record**, opposed Frost's idea and was made a member of a committee to resolve the problem. Because they both were articulate men and represented opposing views, they were asked to write the committee's report. After long private discussion they reached an agreement: Frost would write the report and Gambrell would write the last paragraph—except that Frost would write the last sentence. Following is the remarkable last paragraph written by Gambrell and the last sentence written by Frost (in boldface).

"In conclusion your committee, in its long and earnest consideration of this whole matter in all its environments, have been compelled to take account of the well known fact, that there are widely divergent views held among us by brethren equally earnest, consecrated and devoted to the best interest of the Master's Kingdom. It is therefore, recommended that the fullest freedom of choice be accorded to every one as to what literature he will use or support, and that no brother be disparaged in the slightest degree on account of what he may do in the exercise of his right as Christ's

Southern Baptists meet annually in a national convention. Attendance sometimes passes twenty thousand.

**39**

freeman. But we would earnestly urge all brethren to give to this Board a fair consideration, and in no case to obstruct it in the great work assigned it by this Convention."

This paragraph is remarkable for several reasons: (1) It enunciated the right of Baptist churches to be autonomous even in the choice of literature. (2) It stated that when churches exercise their right of autonomy they should not be disparaged. (3) It asked those who did not accept the purpose of the new agency to treat it fairly and not to obstruct it. (4) It demonstrated the ability of different points of view to find Christian consensus on an important question. (5) It emphatically supported the **one sacred effort** concept of denominational life.

Thus the Sunday School Board was born. Frost was elected its first corresponding secretary, a position he held most of the time from 1891 to his death in 1916. His first years were difficult, partly because the work was new and partly because there were Baptists who did not accept the conciliation of the Gambrell-Frost agreement.

In some quarters Frost was opposed outright, but by the end of his tenure the board was well established and debt-free with its own five-floor building. God's Holy Spirit was working out his great purpose through Southern Baptists' **one sacred effort.** Cooperation was becoming the underlying principle of Southern Baptist strength.

Basically, the Sunday School Board has had two purposes. One is to publish literature and supplies for the churches and their leaders, especially Bible teaching materials. The second is to assist the churches in organizing and expanding their work. From the very beginning Dr. Frost worked diligently at both purposes.

Publications were established in 1891 under the direction of Samuel Boykin, who served until 1899. He was succeeded by Isaac Jacobus Van Ness, who became corresponding secretary upon the death of Dr. Frost in 1916.

Field work was started in 1901 with the employment of B. W. Spilman. Of him Frost said, "He came to Nashville, looked into the little dinky office, and decided to open his office on the field and set up his study in railroad trains along the wayside." Spilman served until 1940 and vastly influenced Southern Baptist churches during a period of rapid growth.

The constructive contributions of the Sunday School Board to Southern Baptist life have been numerous. Some of them are as follows:

1. Bible teaching has been given a permanent and secure foothold in Southern Baptist life.

2. The Sunday School is understood as a primary aid to enlistment and evangelism.

3. All church organizations are under the direct control of the churches.

4. Southern Baptist agencies provide literature and strategy leadership; they cooperate with the states who provide implementation leadership and field services.

5. Teacher training is an important part of Southern Baptist Bible teaching program.

6. The all-age Sunday School is the standard organization for every church.

7. General leadership training is offered by all the churches for all the members.

8. Bible teaching materials are conservative, scriptural, and practical.

9. Bible teaching and leadership training is to be augmented by other services such as church libraries, church music, church recreation, architectural services, and so forth.

10. The Sunday School Board exists as a service to the church and the denomination.

11. The Sunday School Board is a supporter of the vital cooperative concept of **one sacred effort.**

By the time the Southern Baptist Convention crossed the 1900 dateline it had been in existence for fifty-five years. Four great institutions and an auxiliary had been organized, and others had been projected. The two mission boards, Southern Seminary, the Sunday School Board, and Woman's Missionary Union stood proud and strong on the institutional horizon. But most importantly, the churches had been consolidated into a moving, growing denomination. The people of God had themselves become cooperatively the **one sacred effort.** The churches were more independent than ever, yet under God's leadership, and were also more interdependent. All of this was making its impact on the life and the work of the churches and their members.

# The Church as the Family of God

What is a Baptist church all about? This question was asked by a man who came to a church open house at Christmastime. Though he lived in sight of the lovely building, he did not know why the church existed or how it conducted its work. To him it was a building surrounded with cars at certain times of the week. All he knew of its message were its chimes softly playing. There is no record as to how the man was answered.

But there are answers. A Baptist church is not simply buildings and cars or people and services. To describe it in these terms is to miss the richness of its heritage.

Too many people see the church as a building. Baptists are wary of this, and traditionally they have called the place where the church meets the **meetinghouse**. The church itself is something much bigger than a building and much more alive than brick and mortar.

Other people see the church as cars in parking lots, and they count the cars to measure its life. To them the church is hubbub, confusion, and material things. But that is not true of seriously minded Baptists. For the faithful, the church is a gathering of people in a special kind of relationship; and the cars in the parking lot are there only because the church has gathered. Yet the word **gathering** is not altogether accurate; perhaps a better term is **togethering**. Baptists place a great deal of emphasis on fellowship or simply being together in the Spirit of Christ.

The church is not merely people. Rather, it is people committed to a high and holy purpose, people with special experiences and special insights, people under the lordship of Christ. Unless this is understood, the gathering is no more than a gathering in a shopping center or a football game. The commitment of the people is what makes the church truly a church. They see themselves as a family of God, a sacred relationship in which they are drawn closer to each other as an extended family.

When the church gathers, the celebrations and ceremonies mean much more than meets the eye of the stranger. The people gather for worship, a special kind of confrontation with God. This comes in prayer, song, the spoken word, study of the Bible, and fellowship. It provides renewal for Christian witness in the world—Christians gather for worship; they scatter to serve. When the church leaves the meetinghouse, it is as much together in its scattering as it is in its gathering. This is so because of the presence of the Holy Spirit in the lives of the members. In their daily work they have a special appreciation for one another when they meet on the streets or in the marketplace. They develop among themselves love and acceptance that strangers cannot always see or understand.

Gavin Maxwell, writing in **The House of Elrig**, vividly described his boyhood church experience. Talking about an aunt, he said, "I suspect her human horizons, like her interests, were wholly limited by circumstances to the members of her faith, a faith that as a child I shared without question or curiosity, sitting wearily through the age long sermons and services held by tottering old men who had no power to ordain successors."

He wrote of "tired old trembling voices" and prayers that "seemed to be reciting dirges of defeat" and adult choirs that "sang a tempo so slow that all music seemed to be a lament." He described the churches of his childhood as "places of infinite depression and sadness." He said that "unto this fathomless bath of guilt and grief we returned for a weekly dip of four hours."

Is this what the one who came to the open house at Christmas saw? Are church members old people with quivering voices and questionable wit? Have they no meaning at all for their world and their generation? Perhaps a few of them are as archaic and inept as Maxwell pictured, but not all of them. Certainly not all Baptist churches offer a "fathomless bath of guilt and grief."

Take, for example, the very church the man visited for the open house; and take Christmastime as the setting. The long holiday season is a family affair for people of all ages. The church opens its Christmas season with a Thanksgiving morning service. At 7:30 the people enter the sanctuary, nearly as many as are present Sunday morning, and more than half of them youth. After a period of formal worship there is an informal service of song, testimony, thanksgiving, and praise. It is a free and open service with individuals in the congregation taking part. Some read Bible verses; some ask others to sing; some offer words of thanksgiving; and some simply sit and listen.

A list of babies recently born to members is read, and a song such as "Jesus Loves the Little Children" is sung. A list of those who have passed away during the year is also read, with an appropriate song and a prayer of thanksgiving for their lives. But the service is more festival than funeral. There are some tears and a lot of laughter. Love is renewed and the people are strengthened. At 9:15 the people go into the social hall for breakfast. Friendship surely is in that room.

Two weeks later comes the annual Christmas dinner with every available seat taken and people standing around the walls. The program opens with the blast of trumpets and eight men blowing horns and playing Christmas songs as they march through the room. For an hour one happy feature follows another, and then finally comes the worship. Happiness walks out into the night. Even the old and stooped are young in heart again.

Next there is a round of youth events—fellowship, parties, hymn sings, caroling, Bible study, and prayer groups. The youth love the church and give themselves to its work.

Then comes the season of Christmas music, glorious singing by all the children's and youth choirs, and finally the cantata. Some of the songs are written by the minister of music himself. In all of it you can hear youth calling youth. Some are playing violins, some blowing trumpets, some playing guitars, some singing, and ten of them ringing bells.

The pastor is tireless. Beaming, friendly, and young in heart, he silently and effectively leads. Twenty-seven members of the church make about three hundred calls, wishing other people in the community a happy holiday and inviting them to an open house during Christmas week.

The church gathers on Christmas Eve, lifted up to heaven when all the families fill the sanctuary at 7:30 and when for one hour they worship in a candlelight service. The church scatters again out into the night. It goes in the spirit of Christ. Ministry begins again on Christmas morning in the homes and in the community.

As an extended family, the church has within its folds many natural families. This has been true from the beginning. Children

"Let the children come to me, do not hinder them" (Mark 10:14, RSV). These words of Jesus are honored by Baptists who plan much of their work for children.

and youth are always part of the church. Jesus gathered the little children around him and said, "Let the children come to me, and do not hinder them; for to such belongs the kingdom of heaven" (Matt. 19:14, RSV). At Philippi the apostle Paul baptized a jailer "with all his family" (Acts 16:33, RSV). At Troas this same apostle preached to a congregation gathered in a private home. A young man named Eutychus sank into a deep sleep and fell out the window (Acts 20:9). Paul wrote to young Timothy, "I am reminded of your sincere faith, a faith that dwelt first in your grandmother Lois and your mother Eunice" (2 Tim. 1:15, RSV).

Some of the great experiences recorded in the Old Testament boldly uphold the family. God created the family in the Garden of Eden. "A man leaves his father and his mother and cleaves to his wife, and they become one flesh" (Gen. 2:24, RSV). The children born into the families were very precious, "like olive shoots" (Ps. 128:3, RSV). They were to be kept from thorns and snares. The wise man said, "Train up a child in the way he should go, and when he is old he will not depart from it" (Prov. 22:6, RSV). Christians understand all of this to mean that they are not "to provoke their children to anger, but bring them up in the discipline and instruction of the Lord" (Eph. 6:4, RSV).

Baptists give the child a place of honor in the church. In the first place they refuse to baptize the child until he has come of his own free choice to accept Jesus Christ as Lord. Baptists will not abuse the child's personal dignity or freedom of choice. In the second place, when the child does come to Christ and ask for baptism, he is given a full vote in the church. His vote does not count for one-half just because he is small; he is not denied the right of vote because he is inexperienced. Rather, the child counts fully in all the deliberations of the church. In the third place, the church devotes a great part of its energies and resources to the child's religious education. During the first week of his life, he is enrolled in what sometimes is called the Cradle Roll. From that day on, the child is the subject of earnest prayers and the object of the church's educational labors.

Baptist parents take a deep interest in the religious education of their children. Festival times provide special opportunities for teaching.

Baptist churches are made of families and they engage in Christian festival—but this is only part of the picture. To know the church's purpose and nature, one must turn to the New Testament.

First, **Jesus Christ is the founder of the church.** He gathered twelve common men about him and under the open skies announced his intention to build his church. Peter had confessed him as Son of God, the Messiah, God's anointed one. This confession, a prototype of all later true Christian confessions, was the first confession of the lordship of Christ. In response Jesus said, "Upon this rock [the believer's confession of faith in Christ] I will build my church; and the gates of hell shall not prevail against it" (Matt. 16:18).

Second, **the church will not fail.** Congregations may dwindle and even disappear, but they will always emerge again in other places with other people and other forms. In its generic sense, the church is a pilgrimage, moving through times and places as the people of God move in response to God's work in the world. Jesus did not promise ease or comfort for his people; he promised only victory. "And the gates of hell shall not prevail against it." Paul described this victory thus: "Unto him be glory in the church by Christ Jesus throughout all ages, world without end. Amen" (Eph. 3:21).

Third, **the church has work to do.** Jesus

said on the day of his ascension, "You shall be my witnesses in Jerusalem and in all Judea and Samaria and to the end of the earth" (Acts 1:8, RSV). At other times he said, "Go ye therefore, and teach all nations, baptizing them in the name of the Father, and of the Son, and of the Holy Ghost" (Matt. 28:19) and "The field is the world" (Matt. 13:38). By "the field" he meant mankind, for another Bible verse says, "You are God's field, God's building" (1 Cor. 3:9, RSV). Bearing witness to his life and his death, to his resurrection and his ascension, is the work of the church.

Fourth, **the church has a special message.** Jesus said, "You shall be my witnesses." This was not merely the egotistical statement of a man who wanted the world to fawn over him. Rather, it was an entreaty of the Great Physician with the power to heal, the call of a loving brother with the power to save from death, the earnest invitation of one eternally alive with the power to bestow eternal life. "Look at me," he was saying. "I have medicine to make you well, and I have abundant life to save you from death." "Come unto me, all ye that labor and are heavy laden, and I will give you rest" (Matt. 11:28). "And I, if I be lifted up from the earth, will draw all men unto me" (John 12:32). Any egotism that man can charge to him is surely discounted in his death, for he died for all men.

This then is the church's special message—Jesus Christ, his total divinity as expressed in his virgin birth, his resurrection, and his total humanity, as

expressed in his life on earth, his death for all men, and his burial in a common grave. He said in the presence of death, "I am the resurrection and the life; he who believes in me, though he die, yet shall he live" (John 11:25, RSV). The man who asked at Christmastime "What is a Baptist church all about?" should understand this. Then he would have the answer to his question.

Fifth, **the church has a special power with which to do its work.** Jesus told the first church, "You shall receive power when the Holy Spirit has come upon you" (Acts 1:8, RSV). He also said, "Lo, I am with you always, to the close of the age" (Matt. 28:20, RSV). The power of the church is the Holy Spirit, God's special spiritual presence with the believers: "Jesus Christ is within you . . . Otherwise you must be failures" (2 Cor. 13:5, Moffatt). Jesus spoke of the Holy Spirit as Comforter (sometimes Counselor) and as the spirit of truth. "He [counselor or comforter] comes . . . to reprove the world of sin and of righteousness and of judgment" (John 16:8, RSV). He said, "When the Spirit of truth comes, he will guide you into all the truth" (John 16:13, RSV). The special power of the church to do its work and to speak its message is God's own power. The man who visited the church in the open house at Christmas probably did not know this, and his life was impoverished because of his blindness.

But there is much more if the earnest man is to fully understand. The New Testament uses a Greek word to denote church. It is **ecclesia.** William W. Stevens says that most of the time "it designates a local assembly of Christian believers." He also says that it is used in a general sense but that "it is hard to ascertain as to whether the local sense gave rise to the general, or the general to the local . . . The main fact is that when we leave the conception of the local assembly the word takes on a meaning that becomes more and more general." Dr. Stevens then goes on to say that "there are certain New Testament concepts of the church too broad to be denoted by one word." He names three of these: the church as the "Body of Christ," the church as the "Congregation of the Faithful," and the church as

The wonders of nature provide abundant opportunities to teach children about God's great creation.

the "Fellowship of the Spirit."

**The church as the "Body of Christ" is a fundamental concept.** Paul says that God "put all things in subjection under his feet, and gave him to be the head over all things **to the church, Which is his body,** the fulness of him that filleth all in all" (Eph. 1:22-23). Stevens goes on to say: "The church is not an institution, such as the home, or the state, or the school . . . It is an organism, characterized by spiritual life. It is alive and dynamic. It cannot be defined in human terms, as simply an aggregate of individuals brought together for spiritual purposes. It is the body of Christ, and believers are to know a common life in the body of Christ. They have been baptized into Christ. They have put on Christ. He is the head of the church; therefore they live under him. They constitute his chosen and commissioned ones, to whom are given the keys of the kingdom." Christ, of course, is the head; but the life of the head also lives in the body. And the body is the way the head does his work in the world.

**The church as the "Congregation of the Faithful" is the inevitable assembly,** the coming together of the body of Christ for proclamation, worship, Bible learning, prayer, song, baptism, and the Lord's Supper. For the Christian, believing is not a strictly private matter, for in believing the individual inevitably becomes part of the congregation of the faithful. Take for example the words of Jesus in John 15:16: "**You** did not choose me, but I chose **you,** and appointed **you,** that **you** should go and bear fruit and that **your** fruit should abide" (RSV). Every **you** in this passage is plural in the original New Testament Greek. Even in the Lord's Prayer (Matt. 6:9-13) Jesus instructed us to pray in the plural: "**Our** Father" (v. 9) and "Give **us** this day **our** daily bread" (v. 11). The church then is a little community living like a large family, deeply aware of a new life within them and gathering to celebrate it.

**The church as the "Fellowship of the Spirit" has very special meaning.** It is first seen in the word **fellowship.** This derives from the Greek word **koinonia** and also means communion, sharing, and participation. Dr.

Frank Stagg says that **koinonia** is like belonging to a family. "It is . . . to participate with others in the whole of a common life." **Koinonia** is a kind of belonging that is "God's gift, never man's achievement"; but it is both gift and demand. It requires not "mere cooperation, which is an easy achievement, even for pagans. Co-operation is in itself neutral as to moral value; bank robbers can achieve it as well as the 'saints' . . . **Koinonia** is not mere accord, being of 'one heart' . . . It is that accord which is possible only in the creative calling of God."

The special meaning of the "Fellowship of the Spirit" is also seen in the words "of the Spirit." A country club or a debating society is not of the Spirit. They do not possess either the special promise of his presence that Jesus made to the church or the experiences of the members that led them into the body of Christ. Moreover, the country club and the debating society are not self-consciously of Christ. Only the church is that; and in this self-consciousness of being of Christ is the worth and the acceptance that make **koinonia.** To expect the man who stood at the door of the church at Christmastime to understand is perhaps too much unless he willingly becomes part of it. Only as he consents can he discover the answers to his own questions—in the intimacy of the **koinonia.** It is a concept so great that Stagg says, "It (**koinonia**) is not out of place alongside grace and love."

The best way to understand the church is to be involved in it—not as a stranger at a cold

**45**

windy door, but as a brother or sister lingering by a warm fire on a winter day, wanting to stay because of a special kind of love and acceptance. Jesus pointed to this special fellowship when he said, " 'Who are my mother, and my brothers?' And looking around on those who sat about him, he said, 'Here are my mother and my brothers! Whoever does the will of God, is my brother, and sister, and mother' " (Mark 3:33-35, RSV). "The idea of the people of God as a new family is inescapable."

As family, the church experiences the same moments of sadness and joy as any household. When an honored member dies, the whole church grieves, the people standing patiently in line to greet the suffering loved ones. A youth is stricken with leukemia, and one by one church members find ways to strengthen the boy's faith and to comfort his parents. Two young people are married in the chapel, and the church is present to encourage them. A baby is born, and his name is announced in the church bulletin. From infancy to the grave, the members are sustained and strengthened by the loving presence of others. For those who give themselves to the fellowship, there is nothing in the world that compares with the church as one's own family.

The church may outwardly change from one generation to another; but inwardly it goes on in about the same way, drawing strength from the risen Lord and finding joy in Christian fellowship.

For example, one hundred years ago an important part of the life of the church was the camp meeting. Families gathered for a week or ten days and camped along a riverbank. A brush arbor was erected, and preaching and prayers were conducted at least three times daily. These were **koinonia** gatherings—Christian family gatherings—and they created great solidarity among the people, giving them abiding feelings of the church as the family of God. Out of these gatherings Baptists developed a deep sense of denominational fellowship and Christian purpose.

Later "Fifth Sunday Meetings" became the practice. Every time a month had a fifth Sunday, the neighboring churches assembled together for a weekend of preaching and singing. The women spread enormous meals and the youth did their courting.

These gatherings were occasions of fun as well as fellowship. Sometimes the fun was not very funny—at least to those on whom practical jokes were played. On one occasion all the children were left asleep in the wagons just beyond the light of the brush arbors. As the preaching continued, some older boys quietly moved the children from one wagon to another. In the dark the parents saw only that they had the right number of children and were startled at home to find that those they had were not their own. It was before the day of telephones in the country, and about midnight the valley rumbled with wagons returning to the brush arbor to exchange the children. It was hilarious only to the teenage boys who hid in the dark to watch the exchanges. In its way, like so many events of the kind, it contributed to a quality of life so different from today. The slow tempo with which the people lived and the intimacy they knew among themselves provided a social matrix in which the gospel could nourish and grow. The churches flourished and expanded, and God's kingdom spread over the land.

In later times the old ways disappeared and new ways took their places. Yet through all of the changes the truth of the gospel of Christ still prevailed, giving new credence to Jesus' prophetic utterance "Heaven and earth will pass away, but my words will not pass away" (Mark 13:31, RSV).

God's truth will always endure, and the church will endure. It will go on as a special kind of people—men, women, and youth in an extended sacred family relationship—people loving each other, people helping each other, and people reaching out to the stranger at the door—all in the name of Jesus Christ.

# The Life and Work of the Church

The man at the door who said he had come to find out what the church is all about is doubtless, in his way, a seeker. He is interested; so he came asking questions. If he is like most people he wants to know how the church does its work. "What are its programs and functions? How are these related to life?"

There are many answers to these questions, almost as many as there are churches. One answer can be summed up in a short, simple sentence: **The church does its work through worship, witness, learning, ministry, application, and outreach.** The life of all true churches is absorbed in these six simple functions.

### Worshiping the Living God

Worship is a primary function of the church— "not mere entertainment, the passing of time surrounded and engulfed by a ritual. It is not mere objective participation in successive acts and events. It is the giving of honor to God, the rendering of "worthship" to our Creator and Redeemer. It is the drawing close to God,

the communion of spirit with Spirit. It is man speaking to God and God to man. It is one of God's greatest means of developing the spiritual life of the worshiper. It is the time of spiritual drinking and eating."

One of the sincerest acts of worship in the New Testament is seen in Thomas' words to the risen Lord: "My Lord and my God" (John 20:28, RSV). It is through such confessions that one truly worships and not through such simple sayings as "There is a God." The possibility and reality of worship are seen in the majestic and mystical words "For where two or three are gathered in my name, there am I in the midst of them" (Matt. 18:20, RSV). Worship is possible because of the spiritual presence of Christ in the gathered assembly.

Worship in most Baptist churches is relatively simple and informal. Generally speaking, Baptists are not a liturgical people—that is, they do not follow a prescribed body of rites that are commonly practiced in all congrega-

The First Baptist Church in Dallas is one of the largest churches in the world. Most Baptist churches meet twice on Sunday for worship.

The Lord's Supper is a dignified and reverent celebration of Christ's death, observed in most churches once each quarter. It is presided over by the pastor and served by the deacons.

tions. Even the most casual observer looking at Baptist life will agree that there is great variety in Baptist worship from one church to another.

The nearest that Baptist churches come to the liturgical service, in the minds of some critics, is the unvarying routine of small congregations of opening a service with a prayer, singing two or three hymns (usually omitting the third stanza), followed by offering another prayer and receiving the offering. After that a hymn or a special rendition by a choir or a soloist is sung; the sermon follows; an invitation hymn and a benediction close the service. Even when widely practiced and seldom changed, this routine could not truly be called a liturgical service.

Sunday morning services of larger churches are likely to be more formal. The opening is usually a call to worship spoken by ministers or sung by the choir. Then follows a hymn with the people standing; then the reading of the Scripture and the morning prayer are often conducted by the minister in charge. Sometimes the choir sings a response; or perhaps a soloist brings an appropriate song. After this the offering is taken, with the ushers gathering for an offertory prayer by one of the ushers. The organist softly plays as the ushers go about the room with their baskets. When they are through they gather at the front for the doxology, with all the people standing. Then follows the anthem or special hymn sung by the choir. After this comes the sermon, the invitation hymn, the pastor's benediction, and the choral response. At some point, usually at the beginning, visitors are welcomed and announcements made. Some churches are more elaborate in their services; most are less so. There is more informality than formality.

Generally, not much kneeling is done in a Baptist church. Some visitors from other churches are impressed with the lack of prayer rails. This practice perhaps goes back to the early times when Baptists were in revolt against all rites and ceremonies as man-made and useless and as means by which people were held in obedience to civil and ecclesiastical rulers. Baptists worship from the heart. They follow Paul's injunction, "Present your bodies as a living sacrifice, holy and acceptable to God, which is your spiritual worship" (Rom. 12:1, RSV), and Jesus, who said, "God is Spirit, and those who worship him must worship in spirit and truth" (John 4:24, RSV).

Preaching is an important part of worship. The sermon is a long and honorable tradition in Baptist life. Most of the world thinks of preaching as a diatribe against wrong. It can be and sometimes is; and certainly the church is clearly against wrong. But true preaching is not only against wrong; it points the way to goodness and life. Preaching that inspires hope is based on the resurrection of Jesus. As Frank Stagg has said, "Only in the light of the resurrection were the earliest Christians able to restudy the Old Testament, as well as the life and death of Jesus, and see new meaning in the death. In order to set forth the death in its true light, the disciples were compelled to tell the whole story of how, historically, Jesus came to be crucified and what, theologically, this meant."

Preaching, then, centers in Jesus Christ as seen in the Scriptures. It deals with biblical passages. It simply tells who Jesus Christ is and what he means in the light of the biblical revelation. Moralistic lectures or proof-texted entertainment are not necessarily preaching. The biblically based sermon is the simple form of public address practical in most Baptist churches. Some are bad; some are exceptionally good. Most are satisfying, especially to the dedicated members who make up the congregations.

The pulpit in most churches stands squarely in the center of a raised platform at the front of the assembly room, sometimes called a sanctuary. The pulpit occasionally has an open Bible on top of it. This central location of the pulpit emphasizes the important place the spoken word has in worship. In most Baptist churches there are no high and low pulpits and no rails separating the pulpit from the people. The pulpit is accessible to all the members: pastors and laymen, women as well as men, and on occasion even youth and children.

Music is an integral part of Baptist life. Baptists faithfully follow the words "Be filled with the Spirit, addressing one another in psalms and hymns and spiritual songs, singing and making melody to the Lord with all your heart" (Eph. 5:18-19, RSV). In pioneer times, before there were organs and pianos, singing was usually done a cappella, unassisted except for an occasional tuning fork or pitch pipe. Later there came the old-fashioned reed organ and then the piano, which today is present in all Baptist churches.

The great instrument of today is the pipe organ or its modern counterpart, the electronic organ. In addition, some churches have chimes or bells. More recently, some have installed handbells and stringed instruments. A few larger churches have orchestras with violins, cellos, horns, drums, and guitars. Above all else in music is the human voice.

Baptists lift their voices in song in praise to God and as an encouragement to others. The children sometimes are organized into rhythm bands. In some churches families can secure a complete musical education just by participating, so thorough is the leadership. All of this making music is viewed as proper because of the great Psalm 150.

> Praise the Lord!
> Praise God in his sanctuary;
>     praise him in his mighty firmament!
> Praise him for his mighty deeds;
>     praise him according to his exceeding
>         greatness!
> Praise him with trumpet sound;
>     praise him with lute and harp!
> Praise him with timbrel and dance;
>     praise him with strings and pipe!
> Praise him with sounding cymbals;
>     praise him with loud clashing cymbals!
> Let everything that breathes praise the
>     Lord!
> Praise the Lord! (RSV)

Prayer, too, is a part of worship. It is offered not merely by the pastor, but by others too.

Baptist churches are singing churches. Choirs are often well trained. Congregational participation is both lively and worshipful. Many churches have at least one youth choir; some have several.

One thing outsiders have difficulty in accepting is an informal invitation from the pulpit such as "Brother Smith, will you lead us in prayer?" They find lay prayers sometimes stumbling and unclear. Yet in many Baptist churches it is considered an essential part of the worship. Lay prayer can be the spontaneous expressions of Christian experience and, if listened to, can become models for the Christian life.

Baptists try very hard to follow the example of Jesus set in the Lord's Prayer by keeping their prayers trustful in spirit and simple in manner and by remembering that in his teachings Jesus emphasized freedom in prayer. Stilted or hackneyed prayers are not the rule in Baptist churches.

**Witnessing for Christ the Savior**

Witness is another way the church does its work. It leads to evangelization and helps the church overcome its enemies and build the kingdom of God. John on Patmos heard the angel describe the Christians who had come through great tribulation: "And they overcame him by the blood of the Lamb, and by the word of their testimony" (Rev. 12:11). What was true in New Testament times is true today. Victory for the militant church comes through preaching Jesus Christ and telling what he means in the lives of believers.

Every worship service includes proclamation, and in most Baptist churches sermons are accompanied with public invitations. Response is generally given in a walk down the aisle to the minister standing in front of the pulpit. The invitation is given even when none are present to respond. This is to emphasize the always-open door of the gospel.

Witness is also done in special revival meetings held in the church houses or in tents, in rented halls, in shopping centers, and in other places. It is occasionally done on streets, though a much more effective form of public proclamation has taken the place of street preaching—radio and television. Hundreds of Baptist churches have broadcasts, ranging from simple Bible teaching to elaborate multi-camera television productions.

The best witness is face-to-face personal testimony. In this way thousands of people hear the gospel. Conveying Jesus Christ across a thirty- to one-hundred-foot space between the pulpit and the people in the con-gregation is sometimes difficult, and getting through the glass face of a TV screen equally so; but distance melts in face-to-face conversation, especially if the witness remembers the promise of Jesus, "I am with you alway."

The ways of proclamation are endless: printed pamphlets, letters, occasional conversations, deeds of kindness, personal ministrations—and the church ordinances.

Both baptism and the Lord's Supper witness to Jesus Christ. These are the only two ordinances or symbols universally accepted among Baptists. Baptism is sometimes called the threshold ordinance because it is performed as the new Christian stands on the threshold of church membership. Always done by bodily immersion in water on authority of the church, baptism is a simple witness to the death, burial, and resurrection of Jesus Christ and to the spiritual death, burial, and resurrection of the Christian. "Buried with him in baptism, in which you were also raised with him through faith in the working of God, who raised him from the dead. And you, who were dead in trespasses and the uncircumcision of your flesh, God made alive together with him, having forgiven us all our trespasses" (Col. 2:12-13, RSV).

Frank Stagg expresses what most Baptists assent to:

"The act of baptism is symbolical only. The experiences of grace are inward; it is there the spirit meets Spirit. The heart is regenerated and made new in Christ, and a union with Christ is effected. All this is expressed or declared to the world in the act of baptism which represents what has previously transpired: the entrance of the believer into the communion of Christ's death and resurrection." Baptism is sometimes compared with the crossing of the Red Sea by the children of Israel—"the outward form of an inner commitment."

Most Baptist churches today have heated baptistries built into their buildings. The candidates are usually dressed in white and are led into waist-deep water by the pastor. After a brief word: "I baptize you, my sister, in the name of the Father, the Son, and the Holy Spirit," the person is gently lowered into the water until the face is covered; then he is quickly raised again. Some churches still baptize in the primitive manner, in open streams or pools; but this generally occurs only in rural areas where such facilities are available. Even

50

there baptism is in good taste and very beautiful.

Baptists who cherish the tradition of immersion find baptism a precious experience, not as a means to salvation, as some others claim, but as a witness to their participation in the death, burial, and resurrection of Christ.

In most Baptist churches the Lord's Supper is conducted quarterly, also as a way of proclaiming the gospel. Some conduct it monthly. The ordinance came from Jesus Christ himself. In the upper room the evening before his death, he broke bread and drank wine with his disciples, saying of the bread, "Take, eat: this is my body" (Matt. 26:26, RSV), and of the wine, "Drink of it, all of you, for this is my blood of the covenant" (Matt. 26:27-28, RSV). In Baptist churches today the Lord's Supper is presided over by the pastor and served by the deacons. The bread is a small unleavened wafer, either bought at some church supply store or specially baked by the women of the church. The wine is ordinary sweet, unfermented grape juice served in tiny glass cups. In Baptist churches the Lord's Supper is a simple, quiet service, as unpretentious as possible, soul searching, and provocative of deepest inner thoughts. It is a moving witness to the gospel.

The Lord's Supper is a function of the assembled church. There is no occasion recorded in the New Testament when the Lord's Supper was celebrated privately in a family or by a believer alone, at any sickbed, or at any place apart from the congregation of the faithful. It was never intended to be administered as an individual act. "The Lord's Supper is a church rite, to be observed by the assembled church."

**Learning the Holy Scriptures**
A Baptist church is a center of learning—not general learning but a very special kind of learning—Bible learning. The faithful Baptist church tries to avoid a moralistic approach to moral truth. It strives instead to study the whole Bible and to let its higher truths shape the morals of its people. Contrary to what the stranger at the door may think, a Baptist church does not major on "thou shalt nots." Rather, it majors on the great positive teachings of the Bible such as "God is a Spirit, and they that worship him must worship him in spirit and truth" (John 4:24), "God is light,

and in him is no darkness at all" (1 John 1:5), "God is love; and he who dwelleth in love dwelleth in God, and God in him" (1 John 4:16), and "God was in Christ, reconciling the world unto himself, not imputing their trespasses unto them" (2 Cor. 5:19). Of course, a faithful Baptist church speaks against wrong; and it does appropriately teach the "thou shalt nots" of the Ten Commandments. It faithfully tries to set all of these great truths in a clear light.

To do this the church conducts a learning program for all the members and their families. It provides an all-age Sunday School for Bible learning. In recent years the general public has rediscovered the small-group concept for personal Christian learning and involvement, but for Baptists small groups are not new. From the beginning of Baptist life there have been tiny bands of compatible people studying the Bible. In frontier days some of these groups met under trees or in tiny log cabins. Today there are still the little groups meeting in buildings, some of them very large and with many rooms.

The average Baptist Sunday School class for adults has only about ten or twelve members; youth and children's classes are even smaller. In the classes, even though teachers may not always be educationally skilled, real learning takes place. Most lessons are conversationally taught. The members are faithful to these classes. Parents realize that in Bible learning, their children develop strength of character. Children need as much contact with other adults as possible; Sunday School provides that contact. Most adults find a satisfying personal spiritual development in Bible learning. And every earnest Baptist knows that it is through the Sunday School that new Christians are enlisted.

The Sunday School is reinforced by other means of Christian development.

• During the year special weekday classes for Bible studies are conducted, sometimes on church premises, at other times in the homes of the people. These are led by the church minister or by invited specialists.

• Each summer most Baptist churches conduct a Vacation Bible School of one or two weeks for youth and children.

• Churches join together for adult retreats and youth camps which major on Christian renewal and Bible study.

• On Sunday nights most churches gather

Until the era of Reconstruction, most Southern Baptist churches were racially integrated. In recent years many black persons have been received into Baptist churches. More and more black congregations are affiliating with local Southern Baptist associations; and in some cases they send messengers to state and national conventions. The SBC recently had a black vice-president.

for special Bible-related studies. These programs are known as "Church Training" and offer a large variety of study subjects. They are generally planned for all ages.

• The Convention offers a large number of special correspondence courses for Bible learning.

• Sometimes churches conduct special meetings to emphasize such things as family life development.

• Most churches have small libraries of Christian and general books. In some congregations these are called "learning centers" and are well equipped with appropriate books and with other media such as records, tapes, posters, pictures, and audiovisuals.

The object of all Bible learning is not merely to learn about the Bible. Rather, it is to learn the central truth of the Bible, and for Christians this means one thing—Jesus Christ. When he said, "Ye shall know the truth, and the truth shall make you free" (John 8:32) he was speaking of himself—not as a vain, self-praising ego, but as God's final word of love to man. "I am the way, the truth, and the life" (John 14:6).

Perhaps the stranger at the door, wanting to know what the church is all about, does not know because he does not know what Christ is all about. He has not caught the great vision. "In the beginning was the word (Christ), and the Word was with God, and the Word was God. . . . in him (Christ) was life, and the life was the light of men" (John 1:1-4).

**Ministering to Human Needs**
The brief three-year ministry of Jesus Christ can be summed up in three words: worshiping, teaching, and ministering. He worshiped God in constant prayer. He taught the people about God, about himself, and about them-

selves. He ministered daily to the needs of people. He did this whether they deserved it or not, and he used his ministerings as ways of opening their eyes to the love and healing of God. The important thing to him was not their sinful past but their faithful future. He suffered when others suffered and was willing to forget any sin, provided there was a willingness on the part of the sinner to renounce the sin and to face the future with faith in God.

He came to the world to relieve people of guilt, to free them for abundant life and abundant ministry.

The extent of his ministry to persons is summed up in Matthew 25:34-46. He identified with the suffering. "I was an hungered, and ye gave me meat: I was thirsty, and ye gave me drink: I was a stranger, and ye took me in: Naked, and ye clothed me: I was sick, and ye visited me: I was in prison, and ye came unto me" (vv. 35-36) and "Inasmuch as ye have done it unto one of the least of these . . . ye have done it unto me" (v. 40).

Because of Jesus' words Baptists believe that as members of the body of Christ, they too should minister to people in need, both to those of their own congregations and to others, even to strangers. Such ministries are both personal and organized. Some examples of personal ministry are:

• A woman uses her washing machine to wash the linens of the aged sick in the community.

• A man does small repairs for the sick and infirm in his neighborhood.

• A family personally prepares and distributes Thanksgiving baskets to the poor of the community.

• The members of a Sunday School class clean house and prepare food for a family grieving over the loss of a loved one.

Some examples of organized ministries performed by churches are:

• A church maintains a benevolent fund for members and others in deep financial need.

• When tragedy strikes a household and the father is totally paralyzed in an automobile accident, a men's Bible class gathers an offering to help the family.

• A church buys toys for all the children of a children's home at Christmastime.

• The churches participate through their offerings in a large number of cooperatively owned children's homes, homes for aging, and rescue homes.

• A church organizes an elaborate ministry for the aged, especially for those unable to help themselves.

• A relief fund is administered by the pastors for strangers who are in need.

## Applying Truth in Daily Life

Most Baptists believe they have obligations to promote justice in the world. They base these convictions on such passages as the Sermon on the Mount and the letter of James. They believe the words "He hath shewed thee, O man, what is good, and what doth the Lord require of thee, but to do justly, and to love mercy, and to walk humbly with thy God?" (Mic. 6:8). Taking a hint from Thomas Helwys, Baptists do not retreat from service to the community; nor do they isolate themselves behind walls from the problems of the world. Instead they move headlong into community affairs and participate in community institutions, believing with James that "pure religion and undefiled before God and the Father is this, To visit the fatherless and widows in their affliction, and to keep himself unspotted from the world" (Jas. 1:27). Some examples of their involvement are:

Thousands of Baptist young people have served as short-term missionaries—some for their summer vacation, others for two-year terms. They go everywhere witnessing for their faith and making friends for the churches. Music is an important part of their testimony.

Church membership begins with baptism that is administered only to those who openly profess faith in Jesus Christ. Following the example of Jesus, baptism is by immersion.

- A church organizes a community conference to deal with violence on television.
- A church encourages its leaders to participate actively in local politics and even to offer themselves as candidates.
- A church publicly recognizes the members involved in public life.
- A church publicly recognizes the public-school teachers in its congregation and praises them for their work.
- A church joins with other churches in a fight against pornography and neighborhood saloons.
- A church conducts institutes on marriage and family life and offers counseling to people in marital and familial distress.
- A church offers its facilities to Alcoholics Anonymous and other organizations concerned with chronic alcoholism.
- A church takes a stand against the vicious cancerlike tenacles of gambling; it strikes out against organized crime and other forms of criminal injustice.
- A church encourages its members to be good citizens by voting, doing jury duty, supporting qualified political candidates, and performing other similar actions.
- A church refuses to accept financial aid from the government in such forms as funds for church schools, small favors from state and county governments, and outright financial appropriations for church projects.
- A church joins with other churches in forming a private board to undertake housing for the indigent aging and poor.

### Reaching Out to the Whole World

A local Baptist church is never assured that it will always be as large as it is at the present, that it will remain in its same locality, or that it will even continue to exist. Local churches are not inevitably permanent. Only the church in the general sense lives on and on. While it is true that the First Baptist Church of Providence, Rhode Island, organized in 1638, is still in existence, the First General Baptist Church of London long ago ceased to exist. Southern Baptists now have about thirty-five thousand local congregations. Thousands more that once existed are now only memories to a few older people and have no life except in history books.

To view a church in this way is not fatalism. Rather, it is to testify to its pilgrim nature and to point to two important facts: (1) The church grows through evangelism, but (2) the churches grow through multiplying themselves. Both evangelizing and congregationalizing are necessary for outreach. A church must evangelize, and it must establish other churches.

Baptist evangelism is personal through individual witness—one person presenting the claims of Jesus Christ to another. It is also public by means of preaching—almost always in the services of the church, but occasionally in crusades and on radio and television. Baptist parents usually accept the obligation of teaching their children the way of the gospel and of gently leading them to accept Christ.

Some churches are more evangelistic than others. They conduct organized visits to the unenlisted and organize bus routes to gather people who otherwise would not attend.

A few churches hold all their members to themselves, growing larger and larger and providing them more and more elaborate per-

Most modern Baptist churches have baptismal pools. A few still perform outdoor baptisms in running streams where they are available. The Lord's Supper is usually not served to persons until they have made professions of faith and have been baptized.

sonal services. Others believe the best way is to make more congregations. Following the example of the 1755 Sandy Creek Church in North Carolina, they grow by dividing. At one time Sandy Creek had nine hundred members, but a few years later only a handful. Within that period it had sent out 125 ordained ministers and organized forty-two other churches. In modern times there are some Baptist churches that have organized almost as many.

From nature there is an illustration of how churches grow. It is a microscopic amoeba called **difflugia.** This amoeba is different from others in that it absorbs tiny grains of sand which emerge from its body coated with a gluelike substance. The sand, by adhering to the outside wall of the animal, forms a tiny house in which it lives. As the amoeba prepares to divide, part of the house is detached and fastened to the new cell. Vital churches grow like this; some of the members and perhaps even some of the monetary funds are detached to form a new congregation. In turn this new one forms still others. This is how churches multiply. A recent study by the Home Mission Board showed that Baptists grow the most where there are new churches being organized. Strangely, the board found, it is the new church that baptizes proportionately the most members; and that is most likely to start other churches.

Baptist churches have other means of outreach. Occasionally they will employ evangelists to work in neighboring ghettos or they will organize among their members mission tours abroad. However, the most efficient and productive way Baptist churches practice outreach into other communities is through the organized program of the denomination. Baptist churches are both missionary churches and cooperating churches. They are at their best when they are helping each other perform significant world ministries, where they stand together in one great sacred effort.

# Churches at Work in the World

Southern Baptists are deeply rooted in American frontier life. Beginning with William Screven, who felt God's call to South Carolina in 1683, they have steadily gone forward into new lands and new towns. With the great American westward migrations Baptists moved in response to God's inner leading to accept new and difficult challenges. No field was too far, no task too hard, and no barrier too great. If God's Spirit led, his providence would surely open the way. First they moved into the frontier South and the Middle West—for example, Shubal Stearns to North Carolina in 1755, Isaac McCoy to Oklahoma in 1832, and Z. N. Morrell to Texas in 1836.

Even before the South was fully occupied, Baptist pioneers set up outposts in Georgia, Alabama, Mississippi, Kentucky, Tennessee, Arkansas, and Louisiana. Their spirit was indomitable. One early leader on embarking from his ship is said to have fallen on the sands of Galveston Island and prayed something like, "O God, give me Texas for Christ or I die."

Later Southern Baptists followed the westward trail to Missouri, New Mexico, and Arizona, and in recent years to all fifty states, even Alaska and Hawaii. The frontier, wherever it lay, has always been the supreme Baptist challenge.

When the old land frontiers disappeared, Baptists caught another vision of new kinds of frontiers. The old smells of brushfires and newly ploughed earth were gone; the new smells were of congested cities. The symbol was no longer the tiny log cabin in the clearing, but a huge housing development crisscrossed with city streets. Baptists rediscovered the greatest frontier of all: not land, but the human heart. Like Jesus who wept over Jerusalem, they wept over the unreached minorities and unchurched millions.

The new challenge was as large and broad as the world itself. More than ever it required the cooperation of all the churches in the Baptist ideal of one sacred effort. The denominational organization—understood as an arm of the churches—became most essential for bold mission thrust.

The wisdom of the 327 delegates to the 1845 organizing convention was again proven, especially the wisdom of W. B. Johnson, whose vision had seen the need for a strong convention with strong dependent agencies. The convention should give room for initiative and latitude in leadership and provide a close interlocking family of agencies strong enough to hold all the interests of the churches together in a single cause. This structural unity exists within the framework of an unusual setting. In Southern Baptist life there are four autonomous organizations: (a) the local church, (b) the district association, (c) the state convention, and (d) the Southern Baptist Convention. The four are formally independent of each other; yet they cooperate in almost all of their work. The latter three are called "general Baptist bodies." The basic organization is the local church, and from it derives all denominational authority. This comes when the local church sends messengers to the annual meetings of the general bodies.

The oldest of the general bodies is the association, the first in the South having been organized in South Carolina in 1751. The second oldest general body is the state convention. The first one of these was organized in South Carolina. The newest of the three general bodies is the Southern Baptist Convention (1845).

The general bodies are neither superior nor inferior to each other. They are the creations of the churches, and they have equal right of access to the churches. They are on the same

**57**

When Baptist pioneers moved into the wilderness they carried with them a deep religious faith. The first (opposite) Baptist worship service in Texas was led by Daniel Parker, January 20, 1834. The service was held on a riverboat.

mission, and they each have their own way of working. They cooperate in serving the churches by helping them carry out their work in the world. The general bodies have no reason to exist except to assist the churches in the fulfillment of their world mission obligation. The denomination is the churches cooperatively at work in the world.

The Southern Baptist Convention does its work through twenty boards, institutions, and commissions known as agencies. These did not come into existence all at the same time, and they were not established until there was need for them. All of them reflect the life and work of the churches. They are rooted deeply in the experiences of the church members and their leaders, as they seek to fulfill their obligations to the commandments of Jesus Christ. Following is a listing of the agencies showing their dates of origin, their location, and how they relate to the work of the churches.

FOREIGN MISSION BOARD (1845)—Organized in the Convention's very first session, this board sponsors overseas missionaries. Richmond, Virginia.

HOME MISSION BOARD (1845)—First organized as the Board of Domestic Missions, it reflected deep-felt need in the churches for reaching the people of the Western frontiers and the American Indians. It has since expanded to include many more home mission interests. Atlanta, Georgia.

SOUTHERN SEMINARY (1859)—Founded fourteen years after the Southern Baptist Convention, it met the need for providing an educated ministry. Louisville, Kentucky.

WOMAN'S MISSIONARY UNION (1888)—Not a Convention agency, yet works closely with the SBC, especially with the Home and Foreign Mission Boards. It is called an auxiliary and is primarily concerned with missions education in the churches. Birmingham, Alabama.

SUNDAY SCHOOL BOARD (1891)—This is the publications and religious education board for Southern Baptists. It was established to meet the needs of the churches for Bible teaching and church development materials and leadership. Nashville, Tennessee.

BROTHERHOOD COMMISSION (1907)—The sixth oldest cooperating group, it was organized to promote missions in the churches, especially among the men. Boys were included in 1954. Memphis, Tennessee.

SOUTHWESTERN SEMINARY (1908)—Southern Baptists' largest seminary, it was the first to offer degrees in sacred music and religious education. Fort Worth, Texas.

CHRISTIAN LIFE COMMISSION (1913)—An ethics emphasis commission, this agency exists to serve the churches in the needs for the teaching and applying of the basic Christian concepts of Christian behavior. Nashville, Tennessee.

EDUCATION COMMISSION (1915)—A practical group for coordinating SBC and state convention interest in Christian education, the Education Commission represents the interests of Baptist colleges, seminaries, and schools. Nashville, Tennessee.

NEW ORLEANS SEMINARY (1917)—In the organizing convention in 1845, New Orleans was named as a mission field. Seventy-two years later the seminary was established as a means of training ministers for the lower South and for meeting the needs of French America. New Orleans, Louisiana.

ANNUITY BOARD (1918)—Organized to assist the churches in caring for the retirement needs of ministers. Dallas, Texas.

Frontier revivals brought the conversion and baptism of thousands of pioneers. Among them was Sam Houston, the Texas patriot, converted toward the end of his life in a revival meeting conducted by the famous Rufus C. Burleson, president of Baylor University. Many denominational leaders have been active evangelists.

Southern Baptists experienced a period of great growth between 1860 and 1875, doubling their membership in a fifteen-year period. It was a time of strengthening for the denomination. Some of the progress was due to the moving about of great numbers of Baptists during the Civil War. Baptist doctrine was shared around many battlefield campfires.

AMERICAN SEMINARY COMMISSION (1924)—A cooperative venture with black National Baptists, Inc., it is an effort to supply an educated ministry for black Baptist churches. Nashville, Tennessee.

RADIO AND TELEVISION COMMISSION (1938)—This agency assists the churches in their radio and television broadcast needs and represents them in a national radio and television ministry. Fort Worth, Texas.

PUBLIC AFFAIRS COMMITTEE (1939)—A committee that helps form an inter-Convention Joint Committee on Public Affairs and that keeps alert to Baptist interests in religious liberty and separation of church and state. Washington, D.C.

GOLDEN GATE SEMINARY (1944)—Organized to train ministers for the churches in the far West. Mill Valley, California.

SOUTHERN BAPTIST FOUNDATION (1947)—Primarily an agency to hold endowments and other capital funds on behalf of the SBC agencies, the Foundation assures the churches that all such financial resources will be responsibly handled. Nashville, Tennessee.

HISTORICAL COMMISSION (1951)—An agency to encourage the preservation and vital use of Baptist history. Nashville, Tennessee.

SOUTHEASTERN SEMINARY (1951)—Established to help in training ministers for the churches in the states east of the Smoky Mountains. Wake Forest, North Carolina.

MIDWESTERN SEMINARY (1957)—Established to help train ministers for the churches in the Midwest. Kansas City, Missouri.

STEWARDSHIP COMMISSION (1960)—The newest Convention agency, it provides stewardship leadership for the churches. It also assists in the promotion of the Cooperative Program. Nashville, Tennessee.

Laymen have always had an important part in denominational life. The fifth oldest agency is the Brotherhood Commission, organized in 1907. Its first name was Laymen's Missionary Movement. John T. Henderson served as general secretary from 1908 to 1938. He had been a college teacher of mathematics and served as president of Virginia Intermont College and Carson-Newman College.

The Cooperative Program was launched in 1925. It is the Southern Baptist Convention's plan for gathering money for educational, benevolent, and missionary causes.

In addition, the Southern Baptist Convention has an Executive Committee (Nashville, Tennessee) organized for the first time in 1917, seventy-two years after the 1845 meeting. It first had only limited duties and was mostly concerned with the details of the annual Convention. It was reorganized in 1925 and made the central business committee of the Convention.

The period 1917 to 1950, a little more than three decades, was one of the most creative and crucial in Southern Baptist life. First, **Southern Baptists leaped across boundaries that previously had kept them in the Southeastern part of the United States.** A small struggling state convention had been organized in Illinois in 1907 and another in New Mexico in 1912. Both were composed mostly of Southern Baptists from the traditional South and Southwest. But it was enough to warn of things to come. Suddenly, in quick succession, conventions were organized in Arizona (1928), California (1940), Colorado (1940), Hawaii (1940), Alaska (1945), Kansas-Nebraska (1946), and Washington-Oregon (1948).

In this period several things happened to accelerate Baptist movement and growth. One was World War I, which moved thousands of families out of small towns and off the farms into the industrialized cities. Next was the boll weevil that ruined traditional cotton farming, the principal money crop of the South at that time. Almost simultaneous was the expansion of industrial America. With this came the cheap automobile and abundant energy, which made it possible for people to move great distances. Then came the Great Depression and the Western dust storms of the wheat country to speed up the movement of people into areas of greater job opportunities.

Finally, the movement was quickened with World War II, which drew workers into the cities in great hordes. These migrations increased the people's appetites for **things** so that the period immediately following the war, instead of turning into recession, became the country's greatest era of prosperity. With increased manufacturing and great numbers of people, the day of the great city had arrived in America. This meant the organization of more Baptist churches.

One writer describes the spirit of the great migrations in the following whimsical verse.

### The Boll Weevil

Little gray weevil in a field of green,
Looking for a cotton boll with its white,
    white sheen.
Lost in wilderness of sun and shade.
Searching for juicy stalks to climb and
    raid.
Comical little nose with its turned-out
    ends
With two little sprouts and funny little
    bends.
I'd never guess in a thousand years
This tiny gray bug is a maker of tears.
He ate up our crops, tore down our homes.
He destroyed our hopes, foreclosed our
    loans.
He broke up our banks, fouled up our
    ground.
He pushed many a farmer right into
    town.
This funny little bug with gnawing ways
Spread tears and darkness on our days,
But all was not bad as now we see;
This bug brought us our new factory.
He brought new jobs into the South.
He brought new ways to beat the drouth.
He brought new crops better than cotton.
He brought so much, the old we've forgotten.
With that funny little nose, he pushed people
    around;
He pushed many a Baptist straight into town.

He pushed them up North, he pushed them
 out West;
He mixed them all up and gave them new
 zest.
So here's to the bug, for which we are
 grateful;
Even we Baptists, especially the faithful.
Because in pushing us off farms straight
 into town,
More of this nation we can call Baptist
 ground.

In this period church membership nearly tripled, rising from 2,844,000 in 1917 to 7,072,000 in 1950. It was a day of intensive evangelism. The frontier spirit was at work in the city churches.

Second, in the period of 1917 to 1950 organized promotion came into its own in the life and work of the denomination. It was during this time that the district association became much more than an interchurch fellowship and a doctrinal forum. It became the prime mover in organizing new congregations and developed promotional programs to help the churches strengthen their work. The associational missionary, where such existed, was no longer just a colporteur and evangelist; he was an establisher of churches and an expediter of programs. In this same period state convention staffs began to see themselves as specialists in helping the churches in their ongoing programs.

Third, denominational finances, almost in total disarray by 1917, were stabilized and set on a sound business basis. The first step was the organization of the 75 Million Campaign in 1919. President J. B. Gambrell challenged Southern Baptists "to adopt a program of work commensurate with the reasonable demands upon us." A goal of $75 million was set to be paid by 1925. One year later $92 million had been pledged. In anticipation of this money the conventions and their agencies borrowed heavily against the pledges. But depression came by 1925 and only about $58 million had been paid. The denomination was in debt and almost powerless to do its work. Though seemingly a failure at the time, the 75 Million Campaign gave Southern Baptists a solid foundation for the future, as follows:

1. It provided a pattern for the cooperation of the state conventions and the Southern Baptist Convention in great enterprises.

2. It revealed that Baptists working together can raise significant amounts of money.

3. It stabilized both state conventions and the Southern Baptist Convention institutional structures.

4. It demonstrated that Baptists can speedily succeed in one great forward program when they really want to do it.

5. It established a new pattern of stewardship promotion.

6. It provided an impulse for the swift formation of the Cooperative Program.

Fourth, the Cooperative Program was launched in 1925. In some ways this was a further significant fulfillment of the one sacred effort clause of the 1845 constitution. By 1925 the work was suffering, and in some quarters a sense of hopelessness prevailed. The old plan of unilateral approach to the churches by the numerous agencies would no longer work; some new way had to be found. A group of men and women proposed a kind of permanent 75 Million Campaign to be called the Cooperative Program. It was to have the following features:

1. The state convention and the Southern Baptist Convention would be equal partners.

2. Funds would be channeled from the

Dr. Austin Crouch, faithful Baptist pastor and evangelist with unusual business acumen, served as the first executive secretary of the Executive Committee, 1927-1946.

**61**

LORD of the Universe, GOD of the nations, CREATOR of all that is good and beautiful. We are humbled by Thy goodness. We are challenged by the opportunities before us. Let the stately columns of this building remind us that our lives, too, must be tall and stately. Let the beauty and symmetry of these rooms remind us that we, too, must have beauty and symmetry in our lives: May each window in this building be a map of the world: May each door be an entrance-way to enlarged service.

OUR DEAR HEAVENLY FATHER, we would not forget those pioneers who for sixty-four years have carried the torch of service unselfishly. We would not forget those who carry the torch today: those who edit the publications, those who use the typewriters, those who wrap the packages, those who clean the floors, and may each one feel that his or her service is a service for Thee. We would not forget those over our Southland, from the Atlantic to the far Pacific, who are looking in this direction .. those workers .. those women in the cities, and in the towns, and in the villages, and far out in the country who give their time in order that people might know more of missions, and might do more because they know more... Go with us now, inspire us that we may dedicate ourselves to live more abundantly within Thy will, for we ask it in Jesus' name.. AMEN

Benediction by Porter Routh at Service of Dedication, January 21, 1952

This prayer which profoundly reflects a denominational leader's concern for the men and women who work for the SBC agencies was given by Dr. Porter Routh, executive secretary of the Southern Baptist Convention's Executive Committee, at the dedication of the Woman's Missionary Union Building in Birmingham, Alabama.

churches through the state conventions and SBC Executive Committee.

3. Funds would be equally the property of state and Southern conventions and would be divided fifty-fifty.

4. The Southern Baptist Convention would not instruct the state conventions on the division of their portions; nor would the state conventions instruct the Southern Baptist Convention on the division of its portion.

5. Promotion would be provided by the state convention out of funds deducted before the fifty-fifty division.

6. All other priority deductions would be approved by both Southern Baptist and state conventions.

7. Special designated offerings for home and foreign missions would be allowed in order to give the churches clear choices in support of causes.

The new plan was approved by the annual Convention meeting at Memphis in 1925 and was at once set in operation.

Fifth, the SBC Executive Committee was reorganized in 1925 and given increased responsibilities. In the next few years the Executive Committee did the following to stabilize Convention finances:

1. Worked out Cooperative Program agreements with the state conventions

2. Developed a statement on the relationships of the general Baptist bodies for approval by the Convention

3. Developed a sound business and financial plan for approval of the Convention

4. Worked out a plan for getting the agencies out of debt.

Dr. Austin Crouch, a pastor in Murfreesboro, Tennessee, and the architect of the Executive Committee reorganization, was elected the first executive secretary in 1927. It was some time before the Executive Committee was wholeheartedly accepted as a permanent feature of organized Baptist life. Some leaders wanted nothing to do with a structure suggestive of central control. The opposition was such that for several years Dr. Crouch went to the annual Conventions with his resignation in his pocket. He knew that if a fight developed over the Executive Committee he would be the focal point; and to save the Committee he would resign. By 1946, the year of Dr. Crouch's retirement, the work had stabilized and the life of the Executive Committee was assured.

Sixth, in this period 1917-1950 **the denominational agency structure gained new prominence in the life and work of the churches.** Strong cooperative working principles were developed.

1. One general body would not be superior or inferior to another.

2. SBC agencies would work in close partnership with related state agencies in leading the churches.

3. Generally speaking, SBC agencies would provide national strategy leadership and materials; state agencies would provide field promotion.

4. SBC agencies would work together in coordinating their activities so as not to burden the churches. An Inter-Agency Council was formed.

Southern Baptists have a Bold Mission Thrust goal of preaching the gospel of Christ to every person in the world by the year 2000.

It was on the basis of this framework of understandings that the work of the agencies greatly expanded in the thirty-five-year period. By the late 1950s Southern Baptists were facing a period of accelerated numerical expansion of both members and churches.

**Trained Ministers**

Southern Baptists have six seminaries for the training of their ministers. These are housed in impressive campuses owned and operated by the Convention. The schools are not merely brick and mortar or classrooms and libraries. Seminaries are people—trained and dedicated as teachers, nearly three hundred of them representing all the biblical and educational disciplines traditional in Baptist life. Seminaries are also dedicated students, more than nine thousand of them, including sixteen hundred young women.

The typical dedication of these men and women can be seen in an event early in the life of Southern Seminary. The Civil War had ended and the future seemed uncertain. Early in the summer of 1865 President James P. Boyce conferred with the other professors. "The end of the Seminary seemed at hand. When they all came together, Broadus said, 'Suppose we quietly agree that the Seminary may die, but we'll die first . . .' When the seminary did reopen on November 1st, it was with only seven students. In Homiletics Dr. Broadus had only one student, and he was blind. But it was like Doctor Broadus to give this one blind student the best he had. The careful preparation of full lectures for the blind brother led to the writing of **Preparation and**

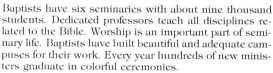

Baptists have six seminaries with about nine thousand students. Dedicated professors teach all disciplines related to the Bible. Worship is an important part of seminary life. Baptists have built beautiful and adequate campuses for their work. Every year hundreds of new ministers graduate in colorful ceremonies.

Delivery of Sermons." This event having as principal characters a brilliant, dedicated teacher and a blind, eager student still typifies the Southern Baptist Seminary situation.

Southwestern Seminary came into being as the result of a day of thinking and praying by B. H. Carroll as he rode a train in West Texas. The vision of the seminary was half-formed. Suddenly it began to unfold to the fullest. The great tall preacher with flowing white beard stood to his feet in the rocking train coach. This is the man of whom a stranger once asked, "Where is your brother?" Carroll responded, "My brother Jimmy? He is at Lampasso." "No," the stranger said, "Your brother Aaron." It must have been an impressive

sight, the crowded railroad car and the preacher standing like an Old Testament prophet, unaware of the people around him and seeing only the vision that God had set before him. Carroll gave his life for the seminary. When he was dying he said to Lee R. Scarborough, his successor, "Lee, lash the seminary to the heart of the Savior."

For each heroic incident known in the annals of the six seminaries there are hundreds of others, unrecorded and unknown, that could testify to the personal sacrifices of the men and women who have kept them alive. The spirit and dedication of Southern Baptist life reflects the spirit and dedication of the teachers and students of the seminaries.

## Baptist Colleges and Schools

The oldest school in Southern Baptist life still in existence is Georgetown College, first established in 1798 as Rittenhouse Academy and reestablished in 1829 under the present name. It is the direct result of the missionary preaching of Luther Rice, who appeared at Mountain Pleasant near Nicholsville, Kentucky, in the summer of 1828. The school was also looked upon as a means of enlightening the Baptist people against certain antimission attacks. Its principal functions were the training of ministers for the churches and the education of other young people for the professions.

In the century that followed, hundreds of Baptist schools were organized in the South and Southwest. Many of them flourished for a time and then disappeared. Some lived and became great institutions of higher learning, as good as any in the land. As late as 1977 there were seventy Baptist schools and colleges enrolling over 140,000 students. Some of them have schools of medicine, dentistry, pharmacy, and law; and many offer graduate degrees in all of the major disciplines.

The largest is Baylor University in Waco, Texas. It was chartered in 1846 while Texas was still a republic. Three strong men were its founders. They were Judge R. E. B. Baylor, an attorney who combined preaching with law, and William Milton Tryon and James Huckins, two missionaries of the American Baptist Home Mission Society. "In his **A History of Texas Baptists** James Milton Carroll says that Tryon and Baylor, making application for the charter, realized that no name had been selected for the new school. Baylor urged the name Tryon because the idea of a Baptist University in Texas had originated with Tryon, also its strongest promoter. Tryon insisted on the name Baylor; and over Baylor's protest Tryon, who held the pen, wrote, 'Baylor University' into the charter." In 1977 Baylor reached an enrollment of over thirteen thousand students. Its campus was valued at about $57 million, and it held in endowment funds about $45 million.

Not all Southern Baptist schools are large four-year colleges. Some are junior colleges and some are small academies. One of the smallest is Fruitland Baptist Bible Institute,

an isolated mountain school in North Carolina. It has an annual enrollment of about 250. Fruitland offers specialized training for ministers who have not attended college. Located in the mountains, it serves ministers in North Carolina, Georgia, Tennessee, and Virginia.

In between the largest and smallest schools is a long list of institutions that form an important part of the American educational system. They are supported by Baptists both through gifts by the churches and special endowment gifts by individuals. Few of them accept federal or state government aid for building construction or faculty support. In this way they maintain their freedom from government interference and a strong witness for separation of church and state.

Perhaps more than any other single force except the churches, Baptist colleges have maintained a high profile for organized Baptist life. Because of them the multitudes have felt the strength and seen the vision of the Baptists.

College buildings are easily identified. Their names are constantly in the papers, and their

The schools and colleges maintained by Southern Baptists are usually owned and controlled by the state conventions. They offer first-rate education in a Christian setting.

Southern Baptists' largest school is Baylor University in Waco, Texas. It was named by William Tryon, who wrote the name **Baylor** in the charter. Judge R. E. B. Baylor protested, but it was Tryon who held the pen.

State Baptist conventions maintain a great variety of programs. One of these is evangelism, which is conducted in all kinds of settings to reach people in different walks of life. These programs are paid for out of Cooperative Program funds and state missions offerings.

graduates are among the leaders of the land. They have given their students as missionaries and ministers. They have stood for justice for all people and have rejected all forms of government interference in the lives of the churches. As much as any other influence in Baptist life, the colleges have contributed to the strength and success of the Baptist cause.

## State Conventions

"What good are state conventions?" is a question often heard years ago. At the beginning of this century there were many "antiboard" Baptists who could see no good in organized Baptist work, especially at the state convention level. This was due to the strong antimission sentiment of the times. The state convention was looked upon as the enemy of the churches and of the free movement of the Holy Spirit. This negative view was long ago dispelled by the successful work of state conventions. In the 150 years since the organization of the first one, they have been proved to be essential parts of organized Baptist life. They perform services not performed by any other general Baptist body.

The first state convention was organized in 1821 and the last one in 1970. These two dates mark a 149-year span during which thirty-one others were organized. Following is a list of those in existence in 1978. Also shown are the organizing dates. Note the variety of names.

South Carolina Baptist Convention (1821)
The Baptist Convention of the State of Georgia (1822)
Alabama Baptist State Convention (1823)
Baptist General Association of Virginia (1823)
Baptist State Convention of North Carolina (1830)
Missouri Baptist Convention (1834)
Baptist Convention of Maryland (1836)
Mississippi Baptist Convention (1836)
Kentucky Baptist Convention (1837)
Louisiana Baptist Convention (1848)
Arkansas Baptist State Convention (1848)
Baptist General Convention of Texas (1848)
Florida Baptist Convention (1854)
Tennessee Baptist Convention (1874).
District of Columbia Baptist Convention (1877)
Baptist General Convention of Oklahoma (1906)
Illinois Baptist State Association (1907)
The Baptist Convention of New Mexico (1912)
Arizona Southern Baptist Convention (1928)
The Southern Baptist General Convention of California (1940)

Hawaii Baptist Convention (1940)

Alaska Baptist Convention (1945)

Kansas-Nebraska Convention of Southern Baptists (1946)

Northwest Baptist Convention (1948)

State Convention of Baptists in Ohio (1954)

Colorado Baptist General Convention (1956)

Baptist State Convention of Michigan (1957)

State Convention of Baptists in Indiana (1958)

Utah-Idaho Southern Baptist Convention (1964)

Northern Plains Baptist Convention (1967)

Baptist Convention of New York (1969)

West Virginia Convention of Southern Baptists (1970)

Baptist Convention of Pennsylvania-South Jersey (1970)

Fourteen of the thirty-three were organized since 1940; others will be organized this decade. Their growth indicates the rapid movement of Baptists into the huge metropolitan centers of America. Their vitality indicates their usefulness to the churches. Following are some of these services a state convention provides:

• A way of consolidating the interests and work of many Baptist churches scattered over a wide geographical expanse

• A way of sponsoring missions and educational activities too large and complicated for a single local church or a few churches in a local association

• A show of strength for small scattered churches remote from centers of power and influence

• A visibility for Baptist work which otherwise might be too small to be seen by large numbers of people

• An annual gathering for representatives of Baptist churches in a state or multistate region

• A means for orderly channeling of gifts to state and world mission causes

• A unit of cooperation for churches who have discovered that working together with other churches is more effective than working alone

• A broad base of compatibility enabling the churches to draw members from each other and enabling pastors to move easily from one field to another

• A communication network for Baptist churches widely separated from each other

• A leadership group to assist churches in developing and expanding their programs.

The size of state conventions greatly varies. The largest has over two million members and the smallest about twelve thousand members. They are all organized differently, some with large staffs and complex programs and others with only a few staff and simple programs. Yet,

State conventions sponsor innovative programs for reaching people. Most of this work is done in cooperation with the district associations. One practical way of reaching people in temporary mobile home camps is by a "chapel on wheels."

surprisingly, there is compatibility and cooperation to high degree. Sometimes the larger conventions will actively assist the smaller ones in some of their programs.

Generally the work of the state convention is:

1. To conduct communicational and promotional programs to assist the churches. A vital communication link is the state paper, of which there are thirty-three. State papers have a circulation of 1,800,000. The first paper was **Christian Index** in Georgia, which began publication in 1822.

2. To assist churches in the establishment of missions and new churches in new housing areas and among minority groups; to conduct ministries of various kinds

3. To own and operate institutions where such exist and are feasible, such as schools, hospitals, homes for children, and homes for the aging. The newer state conventions as a rule do not engage in institutional work. Because most are very small, they have found such work detrimental to the more important mission work.

Buildings are a means of ministry. Some are seminary campuses (**upper right**). One is the unique Southern Baptist Convention Building in Nashville, Tennessee (**center right**). Another is the Home Mission Board headquarters building in Atlanta, Georgia (**lower right**).

4. To serve as a stewardship and Cooperative Program leadership group; and in cooperation with the Southern Baptist Convention to serve as a channel for funds that are to be passed on to world missions.

State conventions do many other things. So vital have their services become that almost no one today doubts their importance and necessity. If Baptists in a region were separated and unrelated, they would at once organize a convention. As long as people exist in social and governmental settings like those in America today, Baptists will have state conventions. They are here to stay as an important part of organized Baptist work.

### The Function of Buildings

Just as a church is not a building, so the denomination is not buildings. Yet in both, buildings play an important part. Without buildings Baptists could not conduct their work in the modern setting. Buildings are an expression of substance and permanence. Sometimes they help preserve the cause itself. During the depression of the 1930s Oklahoma Baptists rallied to save Oklahoma Baptist University. Later the state executive secretary said, "It was the case of a building saving the college. At the beginning of the depression the Women's Memorial Dormitory built by the Oklahoma Woman's Missionary Union was new. It was at the time the best building on the campus. So great was the image of this new building in the minds of the

people, especially the women who had helped to build it, that the denomination sacrificed to save the school."

Today Southern Baptist churches have about $7 billion in local church buildings. These range from tiny one-room rural meetinghouses to huge city education and worship complexes. The Southern Baptist Convention has about $800 thousand in fixed assets, including buildings and endowments. The state conventions all together probably have even more. Most of these buildings bear the cornerstone inscription "Other foundation can no man lay, than that is laid, which is Jesus Christ" (1 Cor. 3:11).

A church building does not exist for itself, at least not in Baptist life. Other church groups may have buildings of sufficient architectural and historical significance to justify them as museum pieces, but not Baptists. Their buildings are functional, erected to serve the cause to which they are dedicated.

The local churches are centers of prayer, study, and worship. Most of them are relatively simple and are opened only on Wednesdays and Sundays. Others are multiroomed complexes open every day in the week. Some congregations do other things in addition to worship and study. For example, one large church has a modern institutional kitchen with a dining room that will seat five hundred persons. It also has a gymnasium with dressing and exercise rooms, a library with five thousand books, offices for twelve full-time staff members, a fully equipped television for

e Executive Committee of the Southern Baptist nvention is the general business group for the Con- tion. It does not supervise the agencies, but does ate to them at many points in matters such as busi- ss and financial planning, the Cooperative Alloca- n Budget, general promotion and public relations, d the annual meeting. The Committee is composed about sixty-four men and women elected by the nual Convention. It has about twenty employees. e Executive Committee meets three times annu- y.

relaying church broadcasts to the TV station, a large parking lot for three hundred cars, another parking lot for twelve huge church buses, a clinic for the medical care of indigent children, a day-care center for children of working mothers, and a special mothers' club building for programs for underprivileged preschoolers. In addition, it owns a modern, fully equipped dormitory that will accommodate fifty persons on the state Baptist summer conference center grounds. While there are many similarly equipped churches in Southern Baptist life, by far the majority of them are simple and unadorned. Yet, in their way, even the smallest meet the religious and social needs of their members.

There is no single building that can be identified as the cathedral or temple of the denomination. Properly none can be called the "headquarters." This is because the headship of the Baptist people is not in anything earthly. It is not in a monument, a building, a place, or an office. It is not vested in any person. The headship belongs to Jesus Christ; and he lives in the hearts of his people, not in a building. Paul said to the church, "You are . . . God's building" (1 Cor. 3:9, RSV) and "the whole structure is joined together and grows into a holy temple in the Lord; in whom you also are built into it for a dwelling place of God in the Spirit" (Eph. 2:21-22, RSV).

Denominational buildings have different functions, many of them specialized in keeping with their purposes. Some are college and seminary classrooms, dormitories, and gymnasiums. Some are homes for children and aging with facilities adapted to the daily care of young and old. Some are hospitals devoted to medical care. One is a great radio and television center. It belongs to the SBC Radio and Television Commission and is located at Fort Worth, Texas. A few of the buildings serve as denominational offices, providing space for workers and meeting rooms for the gatherings of leaders.

Now and then people are critical of these buildings, but most of the time they modify their criticisms when they know their functions. Sometimes what seems to be an overbuilt building is not expensive. It only appears that way because of the use of good design, colors, and tasteful decorations. Often it is the stodgy, undecorated building that costs the most money. One critic who found fault with having carpets in a boys' dormitory was amazed to find that carpets were cheaper to install and cheaper to maintain than flooring.

Baptists seldom have the largest and best buildings in a community, but they often have good buildings that are a credit to the life and work of the denomination.

**From Sea to Sea**
In 1845 America was a vast unsettled continent. There were few railroads and no modern

Among hundreds of home and state missionaries are chaplains. They serve in the military, in prisons, in hospitals, and industry (**lower left**). The missionaries are clever in using the natural impulses of American youth. Here the urge to draw on public buildings is turned to ministry (**lower right**).

communications system. The western settlements were scattered along riverbanks and Indian trails. Excitement was in the land—the kind of excitement that accompanies moving people looking for new homes and new opportunities. The men and women who traveled to Augusta to organize the Southern Baptist Convention took with them bright visions of growing Baptist life in the developing communities. They specified in the constitution that in the future the Convention should "elect at each triennial meeting as many Boards of Managers as in its judgment will be necessary."

There was surely faith and vision in that statement. It meant that whatever organization is needed to accomplish the work is how much organization the Convention should have. At that same meeting the messengers authorized two "Boards of Managers," the Foreign Mission Board and the Home Mission Board. The work of the Convention was launched, and there was no telegraph to announce it. That would come later. The first successful telegraph company in America was formed the same year as the Convention.

The Board of Domestic Missions was given the responsibility for missionizing America. It set slowly to work, handicapped by lack of funds and a mammoth task. But by 1873 it was firmly established, and that year its name was changed to the Home Mission Board. In the years since, as America has changed from generation to generation, the Home Mission Board has changed with it, meeting new challenges with new programs and new techniques.

God's movement in the land evoked great visions for home missions. The spirit of the 1880s and 1890s was caught in a paragraph written by Dr. J. B. Gambrell: "Multitudes of peoples speaking strange tongues will flow into this Southland. At first the Northern man with American ideas will come, but he will be followed by men from every nation under heaven. To prepare for, meet, and christianize these millions is the work of the Home Board. Along the mountain vastnesses of the Virginias, Kentucky, Tennessee, North Carolina, South Carolina, Georgia, Arkansas, Alabama and the great coming cities of the South the battles are to be fought within a generation which will decide the spiritual destiny of this country a thousand years, as human affairs run . . . . There never was a time when we needed broader, deeper, more far-reaching plans for our Home Board than now." Today its field is all America, with its tens of millions scattered from the Atlantic to the Pacific oceans.

In its early years it employed missionaries to work directly with Indians and other ethnic groups; but as state conventions became stronger, cooperative working relationships between the two groups were established. Since 1959 the Home Mission Board and the

In Southern Baptist life there are many ethnic congregations like this Haitian Baptist church. Many of these churches have been established under the auspices of the Home Mission Board (**lower left**). This welcome station sign extends Baptist greetings in many languages. Among Baptists there are thousands of pastors and missionaries who speak two or more languages (**lower right**).

Southern Baptist overseas mission work is done in nearly ninety foreign countries. Native workers help nearly three thousand missionaries teach the Bible and minister to the needs of people. Laos is one of the newest and most fruitful fields.

Wherever it is taught in the world, the Christian message as Baptists understand it is the same plain, simple faith taught in the churches in America. Throughout the world, baptism by immersion is the same simple ordinance that Jesus taught his disciples.

state conventions have worked closely together in providing missionaries for a variety of fields. Following are some examples of the ministries of the Home Mission Board.

**Evangelism.**—The Home Mission Board is a board of evangelism, and evangelism permeates everything it does. In this work it has three approaches: evangelism development, mass evangelism, and personal evangelism. It provides leadership and materials and works closely with state directors of evangelism. It emphasizes the church as the base for evangelism and teaches that evangelism is a responsibility of the laity.

**Language missions.**—The board works with thirty-three ethnic groups in America. These include Indians, Spanish, Chinese, Italian, and French. One of the newest is composed of the Indonesians who recently came to America in large numbers. In cooperation with the state conventions, the board employs about eleven hundred language missionaries. Not long ago 220 churches were organized among the ethnic groups in one year's time.

**National Baptists.**—The Home Mission Board conducts significant cooperative ministries with National black Baptists. This includes student work, evangelism, scholarships for ministers in training, and the organization of new missions and churches.

**Church extension.**—As a rule, new churches grow the fastest. They baptize many more people proportionately to their membership than older and larger churches. The Home Mission Board leads in the establishment of new churches. Like evangelism, church extension permeates all the programs of the board.

**Social ministries.**—Mindful of the Christian obligation to help people in distress, the Home Mission Board extends helping hands to such groups as migrants, disaster victims, social outcasts, underprivileged persons, illiterates, and delinquents. It also provides ministries to families and to the aging. It conducts these social ministries in close cooperation with all of its other programs, especially evangelism and church extension.

**Interfaith witness.**—The Home Mission Board keeps channels open between Baptists and other faiths, such as Jews, Catholics, and Buddhists. Where appropriate it carries on an active evangelistic ministry among other faith groups.

Church loans.—In its long history the Home Mission Board has helped thousands of churches buy lots and build buildings. Sometimes it provides expert counsel, and sometimes it lends money. About two thousand churches annually are served by church loans program.

The Home Mission Board does many other things such as pioneer missions, rural-urban missions, metropolitan missions, and associational missions. At one time it worked in Panama and Cuba, but now its work is confined to the states and territories of the United States. The missionaries use every kind of modern communication device to proclaim the same message so vital to the people who came to Augusta in 1845. If those people could see what God accomplished, they would be amazed at the fruit of their long-ago faith.

### Unto the Ends of the Earth

Foreign missions is many things, yet one thing. It is the simple recognition that for the Christian "The field is the world" (Matt. 13:38). It is also obedience of the commandment of Jesus Christ to make disciples of all nations and to teach them all his commandments. It is the answer man gives to the call of Christ to go to the uttermost; it is the following of the Spirit of God wherever he heads. But perhaps the foreign missionaries themselves can provide the best examples of the depth of the calling of God to evangelize the world.

One missionary described his trip into the remote African countryside. He said that he rode his jeep as far as he could to the point where the road ended. He then rode a borrowed horse until the terrain became so rough that the animal was useless. He walked on through the brush, climbing a distant hill; and just beyond the hill he came to a small community in a clearing. There at the end of the trail he preached the gospel. Only the call of God could put that kind of dedication into the heart of a man. Foreign missions is a long journey to the end of the trail, to the last person in the last clearing beyond the last mountain.

A lovely missionary mother told of her experiences when her mission field was torn by civil war. Her folks in America pled with her to send her children to them. She was greatly tempted but finally wrote her parents, "No, for the time at least, it is the will of God for me to

Personal ministry to people in distress is a part of Southern Baptist foreign mission work. In Benin it is providing wells for water. In Bangladesh it is helping the farmers raise ducks for food. In some countries it is assisting in times of earthquakes and storms.

be here; and my children are safest if they rest at the center of his purpose."

A lady missionary doctor working in a hospital that was overburdened with sick people and understaffed with doctors and nurses quietly said, "I will die before I will leave these people." In a prayer meeting she prayed, "O God, help the people at home to see the desperate need here." Another missionary doctor, also a competent dedicated surgeon whose friends at home thought she was making unnecessary sacrifices, said, "Tell my friends at home that I love this country, I love these people, and I am very, very happy."

Many years ago there was a great missionary to Brazil. He spent almost a lifetime on the Amazon River preaching and teaching Jesus Christ. On retirement he came back to America to live. So intense was his love for the Brazilians that he tried very hard to go back into service. Even though he was crippled and old, he made one or two short journeys at his own expense. A few weeks before his life ended he was seen standing on a downtown Dallas, Texas street corner, leaning on his

cane, his head lifted to heaven, and praying for the Brazilians. The strangers who passed by thought he was insane; those who loved him knew that his devotion to Jesus Christ and his mission field made him the sanest of people.

One of the great foreign mission secretaries was M. Theron Rankin, who went to China as a missionary in 1921. Sometimes he made long walking trips into the countryside. Once he came to a village where no foreigner had ever visited. A farmer let him sleep in his barn, and in the night Rankin was literally rooted out of bed by pigs. The next morning he waited for a crowd to assemble to hear him preach. Suddenly he thought of all those ministers back home in county-seat churches with brick buildings and pipe organs and was swept by a wave of self-pity. In a little while the people came and he spoke. In answer to his invitation an old, dirty, illiterate farmer responded and said he wanted to learn more about Jesus Christ. Dr. Rankin said that at once his self-pity vanished and that on that day he truly became a missionary. When he took the old man's hand he greeted him as "Fellow heir, fellow partaker, fellow member" (cf. Eph. 3:6). Dr. Rankin was once asked

what made him a missionary. He replied, "The study of Ephesians 3 under Dr. W. O. Carver." A careful study of the passage reveals the following points:

1. God has a plan.
2. God's plan is for the redemption of all people.
3. God's plan centers in Jesus Christ as Savior and Lord.
4. God's plan is dependent on the churches.
5. God's plan finally will triumph in the end.
6. Every Christian has a part in God's plan.

Many thoughtful students believe that the Southern Baptist Convention would not exist except for the modern foreign mission movement. They think that the growth of the denomination is directly related to the emphasis placed on foreign missions. They sometimes say that if the day comes when Southern Baptists fail to emphasize missions, their momentum will be lost and they will break apart into ineffective regional conventions.

A study of the history of the denomination gives credence to this point of view. In its early years its most successful program was foreign

George W. Truett (opposite), famous Baptist pastor and leader, made a major statement on religious liberty on the steps of the nation's Capitol in 1920. As a service to the denomination, the Sunday School Board printed and distributed copies of this address. The Sunday School Board (below) conducts a complete publications ministry for the churches. It is located in Nashville, Tennessee and serves the Convention's 35,000 churches.

missions. All of its life the Convention has devoted a sizable amount of its total offerings to foreign missions. Many of its churches, especially the older ones, proudly bear the name "**Missionary** Baptist Church." Its sons and daughters have given themselves unselfishly to foreign missions. Today there are nearly three thousand of them in foreign mission service. These people serve in about ninety foreign countries. The annual budget for this work is more than $60 million.

Looking ahead to the year 2,000 the Foreign Mission Board has projected plans that call for five thousand missionaries. This will be only a little less than double the present number. If this seems impossible, then one should remember that in the twenty-five-year period 1952-1977, the number of missionaries went from 832 to 2,715—a gain of 226 percent.

## The Printed Word

From Florida and Maine to Alaska and Hawaii, the thirty-five thousand Southern Baptist churches have many things in common. One of these is the Bible lesson magazine found in almost every Baptist home and studied in almost every Southern Baptist Sunday School class. These periodicals come from the Sunday School Board at Nashville, Tennessee. This large and important board is responsible for all the Southern Baptist teaching materials. They come to the churches as leaflets, monthlies, quarterlies, and books; and they are augmented with church supplies of all kinds. Because of the work of the Sunday School Board, Southern Baptist churches are among the best equipped churches in the world.

In its long history the Sunday School Board has been guided by sound principles that give its work stability and permanence. Its materials are:

* Written by competent craftsmen to whom the cause of Christ is far more important than the craft itself
* Edited by men and women well grounded in the biblical revelation and solidly loyal to

Baptist tradition and ideas
* Styled in keeping with highest industry and academic standards
* Based on the whole revelation of God as given in the Old and New Testaments. The materials are Bible centered and Bible honoring, yet relevant to today's unusual conditions and issues.
* Printed in an economical manner. The board does not print its literature, so it is able to buy the best materials and services at the lowest possible prices on the open market, in keeping with superior criteria and on the basis of explicit specifications.
* Available to the churches at relatively low cost. In some cases, churches buying from other publishers pay twice as much for inferior materials.
* Related to a basic educational pattern in the churches. There is planned affinity between what the churches try to do in their programs of religious education and the materials that are published.
* Conservative without being stilted or archaic. The board publishes its material for the rank and file of Southern Baptists, whom it recognizes as conservative and loyal to the basic Bible ideas.

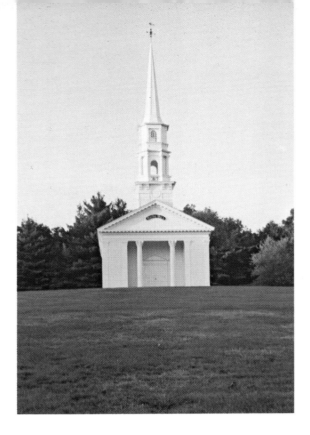

Southern Baptists still have thousands of open country churches. In the years ahead many of these will grow as people move into rural areas. But for some time to come the majority of Baptists will live in the great cities. The future of Southern Baptists' life depends on how well they work in the metropolitan centers.

• Available for a wide range of age groups, including young, median, and senior adults. Available also in a variety of forms to give the churches a choice of curriculums.

The Sunday School Board conducts its work on a sound business basis. It turns the profits it earns from its sales into services performed for the churches and the Convention and its agencies. It also supplements state convention field service budgets and conducts two large national conference centers at Glorieta and Ridgecrest. One of the board's most useful functions is the maintenance of a network of Baptist Book Stores. In some ways the strength and vitality of the denomination can be measured by the support the churches give to the board and its book stores.

## Southern Baptists Today

Some people think that Southern Baptists see themselves as almost the only true Christians. They say, "You insist on conversion before church membership; you hold strict views of baptism; and you have not joined any of the ecumenical organizations." Yes, these charges are true for most Southern Baptists. But while most Southern Baptists have firm convictions, they don't see themselves as ex-clusive among other Christians. True Baptists are willing to receive any person anywhere who has sincerely turned from sin and accepted Jesus Christ as Lord and Savior as a brother or sister in the kingdom of God.

This openness toward all Christians everywhere led the late W. T. Conner, a renowned theologian and New Testament scholar, to say that Baptists are the original ecumenists. They accept any true Christian of any other church group as equal to themselves. They believe, however, that their special views of the church preclude organized ecumenical ties. Southern Baptists especially have never become involved in organizations that would compromise their distinctiveness and independence. Events of recent years seem to have proved the correctness of this position.

Southern Baptists are certainly not the only Baptists in the world. In America there are twenty-three other organized Baptist groups. These range in size from a group as small as the Duck River and Kindred Associations of Baptists with less than 100 churches and 10,000 members to one as large as the National Baptist Convention, Inc. with about 26,000 churches and 5.5 million members. In the United States there are about 99,000 Baptist churches with 19 million members. The totals for the world are about 137,000 churches with 33 million members.

There is a Baptist witness in almost every country in the world. One of the most vigorous Baptist fellowships is in Russia, where there are about 230,000 counted members and probably a great many more uncounted ones. Most of these Baptists work together in an international fellowship known as the Baptist World Alliance. This group meets in an international congress every five years.

Southern Baptists grew faster in the postwar years than at any time in recent times. From 1945 to 1960 they added nearly four million members, a gain of about 65 percent. In this same fifteen-year period they added over six thousand churches, a gain of about 24 percent. There were many factors responsible for this great growth.

In America it was a time of change. People were moving into new jobs and new homes. Families were multiplying. There was an unprecedented birth rate. Southern Baptists practiced a fervent evangelism, and the church programs were simple and uncluttered. Strong leaders were in charge of the programs. The simplicity of life made face-to-face communication easy and effective. There was not the fierce competition of media there is today; and mass sports and mass recreation were not priorities among people.

## Southern Baptists Tomorrow

There is no way to return to the postwar years. To try to recreate the opportunities and methods so vital then would be a foolish reactionary exercise today. Important as it is to look backward to understand oneself, it is wrong to try to reduplicate the old times.

Rather, Southern Baptists must ask, "What are our opportunities now? What can we do today and tomorrow?" New objectives and new ways of working must be found for the new times.

The churches must extend or perish.

They live in a biblical milieu, and they must derive their dynamics from a clear understanding of the Scriptures.

Leadership in extension is imperative, and the pastor is the leader. He sets the example in evangelism and equips others to follow his example. He leads the church to dream new tasks, even to attempt the impossible, knowing that with God all things are possible. Under his leadership the laity is trained, and all the "spectators become participants."

The ways the denomination and the churches are organized must themselves become channels for conquest. If organizations cannot contribute to the life of the church, they should be discontinued. In other words, one does not fit strategies to the system but makes the system itself a strategy.

People must be awakened, quickened, and developed. The great dream of winning the whole world to Christ must come true. The new agenda calls for the churches to:

- Set goals for church member involvement in evangelism and missions

- Conduct a strong person-to-person evangelism
- Organize and carry out aggressive small-group Bible teaching programs in church buildings, in homes, and wherever there are clusters of compatible people
- Conduct multiple and varied ministries in the churches to reach persons of different backgrounds and interests
- Organize new missions and churches where people are brought together for witness and ministry
- Broaden the understanding of church members of the biblical basis and practical understanding of missions

The growing edge of the denomination will not be some esoteric and innovative method. Rather, it will be the use of proven basic methods such as person-to-person evangelism and small-group Bible study (upper). The Bible study of tomorrow will be conducted both in church buildings and in other places where compatible groups are found (lower).

• Involve church members in active evangelistic and mission work

• Conduct systematic, effective planning to accomplish the tasks most essential to the continued vitality of Southern Baptist life.

The churches exist as the body of Christ in the world. Because they are in Christ and he is in them, they should show his love to all people. "He who does not love does not know God; for God is love" (1 John 4:8, RSV).

The churches, then, are to be centers of love, so attractive that all people will be drawn to them. Once a man was sitting in a circus when performers dressed like apes ran from the arena into the stands. Some of the children were frightened, and for a moment the situation was so unreal that the man himself was frightened. He felt something warm against

The Baptist work of tomorrow will require varied ministries such as mission work among youth (**right**), witness and ministry to the unfortunate members of society (**below**), ministries to the aging, mission action by missionary organizations (**lower right**), and highly sophisticated approaches through radio and television (**lower left**). It will also require programs of social service and Christian citizenship. A solid emphasis on ethics will play a large part in tomorrow's Baptist work.

his arm and looked to see a tiny four-year-old boy trying to hide behind him. The man lifted his arm and the boy snuggled under it. Soon the child's tears were dried and he was laughing. The man thought, **The world is frightened and needs an arm of love and protection.** If only the church could be that arm to draw into itself the people who stand crying at its doors! Their tears would cease, and laughter would come again. Only when the churches truly love will the world be attracted and saved from its sin. Whatever message the churches speak, through it the world must see and experience the love of God.

Life in the world is changing, but this is not new. In one generation there were horses and wagons, and in the next there were cars and trucks. In the generations ahead there will be something still different. The ways people organize their homes and conduct their work are subtly altered as time passes.

But some things do not change—the sufferings of brokenhearted people, the outrages of sin, and the guilt and destitution of sinners. Human need does not change. Wrong must be made right; error must give way to truth; and guilt must become forgiveness. Wherever there are broken hearts and broken lives, wherever there is hunger and thirst for righteousness, wherever there is the need for cleansing from unrighteousness—precisely there is where the church must work in the world. Southern Baptists understand this, and they see the whole world as their field.

So in these days when so much is changing they have concluded that they have much to give. In the last twenty-five years of the twentieth century Southern Baptists have set for themselves a major BOLD MISSION THRUST objective.

It is that every person in the world shall have the opportunity to hear the gospel of Christ in the next twenty-five years and that in the presentation of this message the biblical faith be magnified so that all men, women, and children can understand the claim Jesus Christ has on their lives.

• This task calls for five thousand foreign missionaries by the year 2000.

• It calls for a vital reactivation of local associational missions.

• It calls for increased home and state mission work.

Youth are the Baptist hope for tomorrow. They have an important part in Bold Mission Thrust and the Mission Service Corps. The archives of the SBC Historical Commission of the next generation will be filled with stories of their Christian deeds. Grandchildren of today's Baptists will read of the heroic works not yet performed but as great as those of Thomas Helwys, Shubal Stearns, and others like them.

• It calls for thousands of volunteers to serve in short-term mission work. For example, five thousand **Mission Service Corps** workers will go to various places of service almost immediately. They will serve partially at their own expense. Many will be retirees, and some will be youth. Thousands of others will help support them.

To some people this seems an impossible dream. But long ago Thomas Helwys crossed the English Channel with a dozen Baptists to face the fury of the English persecutions. Later Shubal Stearns went in wagons with eight families to face the wilderness challenge of North Carolina. These Baptist pioneers dreamed of the tasks that God set before them, not of the impossibilities. So Baptists today must dream of the tasks God has set before them and remember that with God all things are possible. "This is the victory that overcometh the world, even our faith" (1 John 5:4).

**81**

## Acknowledgment

Broadman Press expresses thanks to Mrs. Vernon (Peggy) Elmore, who suggested this publication.

## Illustrations

The editorial staff of **Meet Southern Baptists** gratefully acknowledges the kindness of the institutions and agencies listed, who have given their permission for us to reproduce their art.

Paintings are by: Al Buell (p. 46—Baptist Sunday School Board); Erwin M. Hearne, Jr. (pp. 13, 18, 22, 25, 26, 36, 76—Baptist Sunday School Board; pp. 32, 35, 56, 58, 59 upper right, 66—Baylor University; 59 lower right—Brotherhood Commission); Robert Heuell (pp. 6, 9—Baptist Sunday School Board); Richard Hook (pp. 7, 10, 43, 44, 45, 54, 55 upper right, 55 lower right—Baptist Sunday School Board); Harold Minton (p. 5—Baptist Sunday School Board); Executive Committee (p. 39); Foreign Mission Board (p. 27 center); Home Mission Board (p. 33); Southern Baptist Theological Seminary (pp. 34, 38 lower left); Southwestern Baptist Theological Seminary (pp. 31, 38 upper right).

Photographs are by: Jimmy Allen (p. 53—Home Mission Board); Doug Brachey (pp. 30, 61, 77 lower right—Baptist Sunday School Board); Bob Churchwell (p. 68—Baptist Sunday School Board); Rachel Colvin (pp. 63, 80 lower left—Radio and Television Commission); Richard Dodge (p. 65 left—New Orleans Baptist Theological Seminary); Toby Druin (p. 72 left—Home Mission Board); William R. Estep, Jr. (pp. 11, 24 upper left); Ben Fisher (p. 42—Education Commission); Larry Goddard (p. 79 upper—Home Mission Board); Bill Grimes (pp. 48, 73 left—Home Mission Board); Chris Hansen (pp. 32, 35, 36, 58, 59 upper right, 66—Baylor University); Everette Hullum (p. 72 right—Home Mission Board); Randy Miller (p. 79 lower—Home Mission Board); Andrew Rawls (pp. 27 upper, 31—Southern Baptist Theological Seminary); Don Rutledge (pp. 15, 52, 69, 70 lower, 73 right, 78—Home Mission Board); Orville Scott (p. 47—Home Mission Board); Lawrence Snedden (p. 27 lower right—Foreign Mission Board); Annuity Board (p. 80 lower right); Baptist Sunday School Board (p. 3); Brotherhood Commission (p. 80 upper right and center left); Executive Committee (pp. 49, 60, 64 center left, 70 center, 71); First Baptist Church, Providence, Rhode Island (p. 14); Foreign Mission Board (pp. 27 lower left, 74 upper and lower, 75); Southeastern Baptist Theological Seminary (p. 64 lower right); Southern Baptist Theological Seminary (pp. 64 center right, 65 right); Southwestern Baptist Theological Seminary (p. 70 upper); William Jewell College (p. 67); Woman's Missionary Union (pp. 62, 80 far lower right, 81).

Drawings are by: W. Robert Hart (p. 24 lower right—Foreign Mission Board); Erwin M. Hearne, Jr. (pp. 17 upper left and lower right, 19 upper center and lower center, 20 upper left and upper right, 21 lower right and lower left—Historical Commission); Ron Martin (pp. 23, 28, 37, 77 upper left—Baptist Sunday School Board).

## Bibliography

Babb, Marguerite Skinner, ed. The Quarterly Review 37 (July, August, September 1977). © Sunday School Board of the Southern Baptist Convention.

Baker, Robert A. The Southern Baptist Convention and Its People 1607-1972. Nashville: Broadman Press, 1974.

Barnes, W. W. The Southern Baptist Convention 1845-1953. Nashville: Broadman Press, 1954.

Chaney, Charles L., and Lewis, Ron S. Design for Church Growth. Nashville: Broadman Press, 1977.

Cox, Norman W., ed. Encyclopedia of Southern Baptists, Vols. I and II. Nashville: Broadman Press, 1958; Davis C. Woolley, ed., Vol. III. Nashville: Broadman Press, 1971.

Hogue, C. B. I Want My Church to Grow. Nashville: Broadman Press, 1977.

Maxwell, Gavin. The House of Elrig. New York: E. P. Dutton and Company, 1965.

May, Lynn E., Jr., ed. Baptist History and Heritage (1965 +) © Historical Commission of the Southern Baptist Convention.

Stagg, Frank. New Testament Theology. Nashville: Broadman Press, 1962.

Stevens, William W. Doctrines of the Christian Religion. Nashville: Broadman Press, 1967.

Torbet, Robert G. A History of the Baptists. Valley Forge: Judson Press, 1963.

Underwood, A. C. A History of the English Baptists. London: Kingsgate Press, 1947.

Whitley, W. T. A History of British Baptists. London: Charles Griffin and Company, 1923.

Woolley, Davis C., ed. Encyclopedia of Southern Baptists, vols. 1, 2, 3. Nashville: Broadman Press, 1971.

THE COVER DESIGN is a variation on the logo of the Southern Baptist Convention. The logo has three elements: The Bible, the cross, and the world. The meeting house in the upper left quadrant represents local bodies of baptized believers. The upper right quadrant symbolizes the task of Christian education. In the lower right quadrant is a communications satellite which represents the churches' task of communicating the Gospel to every person. The tools in the lower left quadrant speak of the application of the Gospel to all of life.

The stained glass window on p. 3 is found in Van Ness Auditorium at the Baptist Sunday School Board. It's a graphic illustration of the Christian message—both word and deed.